The Open University

Business School

Book 1
What is retailing?

GW00600712

Prepared by Fiona Ellis-Chadwick

This publication forms part of the Open University module B122 *An Introduction to Retail Management and Marketing*. Details of this and other Open University modules can be obtained from the Student Registration and Enquiry Service, The Open University, PO Box 197, Milton Keynes MK7 6BJ, United Kingdom (tel. +44 (0)845 300 60 90; email general-enquiries@open.ac.uk).

Alternatively, you may visit the Open University website at www.open.ac.uk where you can learn more about the wide range of modules and packs offered at all levels by The Open University.

To purchase a selection of Open University module materials visit www.ouw.co.uk, or contact Open University Worldwide, Walton Hall, Milton Keynes MK7 6AA, United Kingdom for a brochure (tel. +44 (0)1908 858793; fax +44 (0)1908 858787; email ouw-customer-services@open.ac.uk).

The Open University Walton Hall, Milton Keynes MK7 6AA

First published 2011

Edited and designed by The Open University.

Typeset in India by OKS Prepress Services, Chennai.

Printed and bound in the United Kingdom by Cambrian Printers, Aberystwyth.

ISBN 978 1 7800 7310 1

2.1

Contents

Introduction to Book 1

Welcome to Book 1 which focuses on ideas and theories that should help you develop your understanding of the principles of retailing, the meaning of the term retailing and the environment where retailers trade.

This book is designed to follow on from the multimedia activities in the first study session of Block 1, which is accessible via the B122 module website.

There are three study sessions in this book:

1 What is retailing?

2 Understanding the retail environment (part 1)

3 Understanding the retail environment (part 2)

Now you are studying Book 1, please do not think because it tackles the *theories* associated with retailing that it is out of touch with the real world. Throughout the book, you find real world examples, illustrations, and pictures to help you understand particular ideas and concepts:

The independent and the multinational store

Can you think what might affect both of these retailers in a similar way? The Ennis Bookshop is an independent book retailer that operates in County Clare on the west coast of Ireland. Tesco Plc is a market leading grocery retailer that operates in excess of 4,000 stores worldwide. The answer is that both organisations are affected by forces in the *retail environment*. It does not matter whether it is an independent shop in Abbey Street, Ennis or a very large supermarket operation like Tesco with stores spread across the globe – economic influences, competitors, customers, and other forces that make up the retail environment, affect both operations. It is important to learn about the forces and actors; which make up the retail environment in order to develop the knowledge and skills needed to understand how retailers respond to changes in the real world.

You will discover as you study the module that retailing is a highly dynamic and vibrant subject and is closely linked to our everyday experiences.

Learning outcomes

The main aim of Book 1 is to provide you with a broad understanding of retailing and its trading environment and to:

- provide a working definition of retailing
- explore the concept of customer value
- identify and examine the external forces which affect retailers and make up the retail environment: political, legal, economic, ecological, physical, social, cultural and technological
- identify and examine the *actors* in a retailer's immediate environment, which can affect business performance
- explore the development of retailing and how styles of retailing change
- outline the elements of a retail operation.

Session 2 What is retailing?

This session examines the definition of retailing. We will look at how retailing relates to the concept of customer value and how retailers create and deliver customer value through products, services and stores. Finally we will look at the theories explaining the development of retailing over time.

2.1 Defining retailing

A convenience store is a local store selling a limited variety of products (generally food and other household necessities), which is open for longer hours than other retailers e.g. One Stop, Londis and Spar.

As individuals, we need various goods and services to live our lives, and we acquire a significant proportion of them from specialist providers, for example: foodstuffs from a grocer; birthday cards from a stationer; a meal from a restaurant. These specialist providers generally offer items for sale that are ready for us to use and are for our own consumption. We call these providers *retailers*, and it is the relationship between the *quantity of goods* sold and the *type of customer* served which helps us to define the meaning of retailing. According to Varley and Rafiq:

> The word retailing has its origins in the French verb *retailler*, which means 'to cut up', and refers to one of the fundamental retailing activities, which is to buy in larger quantities and sell on in smaller quantities. For example, a convenience store would buy tins of baked beans in units of two-dozen boxes, but sell in single-tin units. However, a retailer is not the only type of business entity to 'break bulk'. A wholesaler also buys in larger quantities and sells on to their customers in smaller quantities. It is the type of customer, rather than the activity, that distinguishes a retailer from other distributive traders; that distinction being that a retailer sells to final consumers, unlike a wholesaler who sells on to a retailer or other business organization.

(Varley and Rafiq, 2004, p. 4)

Activity 2.1 Personal experience

Spend about 20 minutes on this activity.

Purpose: to help you to think about what retailing means to you and to help you develop your own definition of retailing.

Task: Think about the last time you went into a shop to buy something. Perhaps it was today to buy groceries, or last weekend to buy special gifts for a friend's birthday.

Now make a list of your last five shopping purchases. Include the quantities you bought of each item and the reason for making the purchases.

1

2

3

4

5

Feedback

On many occasions, we routinely go shopping without thought or consideration to what we want to buy or why we are going shopping. Nevertheless, we expect the products we want to be available. Retailers have to anticipate our requirements in order to make the products we're looking for available at the right place and time, in the right quantities and at the right price. To do this, they study and analyse our behaviour to work out how the products they sell will meet our needs.

This task aims to get you thinking about why you buy certain products.

Here's my list of recent purchases:

1   1 can of paint

2   6 rolls of wallpaper

3   1 paper scraper

4   1 set of paintbrushes

5   1 take-away meal.

Why did I buy these products?

The straightforward answer is that I am redecorating my kitchen. I needed the DIY products to complete the job and the food to eat whilst working.

But is that the only reason for buying these things?

No. The underlying reason for making these purchases is to improve my lifestyle. It is these underlying reasons, which prompt us to make purchases, that help retailers decide which products to sell.

I bought the decorating items from a Dulux Decorator Centre, where the product ranges include: paint, wall coverings, accessories, fabrics and soft furnishings. In other words, the retailer stocks all of the products I might use to create better living conditions throughout my home, therefore enabling me to achieve the ultimate goal of improving my lifestyle.

You may find it amazing that retailers know which products to sell to meet our needs and how they generally make available all the products that we want. This is actually an important part of the definition of retailing, and helps us to understand that the modern retailer does more than 'buy in larger quantities and sell on in smaller quantities' (Varley and Rafiq, 2004, p. 4). They study our needs and requirements so that they can present us with what we want, when we want it and at a price that we are prepared to pay. Retailers have not always been so responsive to our needs, as you will discover as you work through the module.

2.2 Understanding customer value

It is difficult to pinpoint an exact date when retailers began to use the principles of marketing to drive their businesses. However, sometime in the mid-1960s to early 1980s there was a definite shift towards satisfying customer needs.

Traditionally, retailing was considered a rather passive activity, with goods passing from the manufacturer to the wholesaler then to the retailer and, finally, to individual customers. Retailers would display available products and attempt to sell them to their customers with limited regard for what the customers wanted. However, eventually, retailers discovered that understanding what was important to the customer meant they could stock the right products, sell at the right price and ultimately *increase profits* rather than having to *push* the products they had in stock, often at reduced prices. The era of 'stack them high and sell them cheap' has ended. Retailers have discovered the importance of *understanding and satisfying customer needs* and this represents an important landmark in the development and definition of modern retailing.

According to Jobber, companies are using a marketing approach when they create:

> ... customer value in order to attract and retain customers. Their aim is to deliver superior value to their target customers. In doing so, they implement the marketing concept by meeting and exceeding customer needs better than the competition.

(Jobber, 2010, p. 13)

The basic idea is that *customer value* is determined by the *benefits* we get less the *sacrifices* we have to make. The problem is that customer value means different things to different people – and this makes it tricky to define.

Let's look at an example. Imagine you want to buy a ready-made meal of chicken curry. Table 2.1 lists some options.

Table 2.1 Chicken curry product options

Product	Average price	Calorie content per 100 grams	Product description: indicator of taste and flavour[1]
Birdseye Healthy Options Chicken Curry	£1.49	99	Tender pieces of chicken in a spicy curry sauce and fine long grain rice.
Tesco Chicken Curry	£1.00	120	Tender pieces of chicken breast in a mild curry sauce served with rice.
Sainsbury's Hot Chicken Vindaloo Curry	£3.29	145	Marinated chicken breast pieces in an extra hot and spicy onion and tomato sauce.

[1] The descriptions have been modified for this exercise.

Chicken curry options

If the key *benefit* you are looking for is *low cost*, then you would choose Tesco's own brand. The *sacrifices* you will make are that the calorie content per 100 grams is higher than the Birdseye Healthy Options curry and that there might be a compromise on taste as the Chicken Vindaloo has marinated chicken breast pieces – implying more flavour.

If the key *benefit* you are looking for is *low calories* you would choose Birdseye Healthy Options Chicken Curry at 99 calories per 100 grams. The *sacrifices* you will make are the price, which is relatively high, and again there might be a compromise on taste due to use of lower-fat ingredients – although we cannot tell this from the product details.

Reflection

Using Table 2.1, suggest the key benefits and the sacrifices if you were to buy the Sainsbury's Hot Chicken Vindaloo Curry.

Feedback

The key benefits are (arguably) quality and taste. The sacrifices are cost and calorie content. This option is the most expensive and has the highest calorific value per 100 grams of our three choices.

Once a retailer understands customer value, they can set about creating it for the customers they want to attract to their stores. Different retailers offer different combinations of benefits to encourage us to shop in their stores. A survey of 36,308 individuals by the BBC consumer programme Watchdog (2009) found that:

- ASDA offers the best value (which means it delivers benefits to its customers through prices)
- Marks and Spencer offers the best quality food (which means it delivers value through the quality of its products)
- Waitrose offers the best overall experience as it was voted 'Britain's favourite supermarket' because of its excellent customer service, high-quality products and good prices (which means it delivers value through product benefits, price benefits and customer service benefits).

Today, retailing means:

- understanding what the customer wants and how to add value
- creating and delivering customer value by developing suitable product ranges and services.

In this section, we have explored some of the broad principles of understanding customer value. Next, we examine ways that retailers create and deliver customer value.

2.3 Creating and delivering customer value

Retailers can create value through the *products* they sell, the *services* they offer, and the *stores* from which they sell. We will now look at each of these aspects in turn.

Products

Retailers should understand the implications of selling particular types of products if they are to create customer value. Table 2.2 (below) shows the range of different product categories and sub-categories a retailer in the UK might choose to sell.

When planning product ranges, retailers consider the implications of selling different product categories. For example:

- Products vary in *value and price*, which from a retailer's viewpoint has implications for financial investment and security. For instance, birthday cards are relatively low value and low cost, whereas diamond and gold jewellery is high value and high cost.

- Products vary in *volume*, which has logistical and storage implications. For instance, a wardrobe requires, say, three square metres of display space, whereas hundreds of musical CDs could be displayed in a similar-sized area.

- Products vary in *perishability*, which has implications for stock holding and stock management. For instance, a loaf of bread has a shelf life of a few hours whereas fine wines and spirits can be stored for years.

- Products vary in *tangibility*. Items such as clothing, furniture, and foodstuffs are physical goods, which we can touch, feel and carry home. Products such as insurance and beauty treatments are intangible products, which we benefit from but cannot hold in our hands.

Table 2.2 Retail product categories (in the United Kingdom)

Category	Sub-category
Alcohol	Wines, beers, spirits
Books and stationery	Printing, cards, paper, pens, writing materials
Chemists and drugstores	Beauty products, toiletries, cosmetics
Clothing	Baby wear and nursery goods, children's wear, ladies' wear, men's wear, knitwear, fashion accessories, work wear, school wear, maternity wear, lingerie, leather wear, sports wear, bridal wear
DIY goods	Wallpaper, paint, hardware, ironmongery, doors

Electrical goods	Computer hardware, computer software, white goods, brown goods, audio-visual
Finance	Banking, insurance, credit, building societies
Footwear	Children's, ladies' and men's shoes, sports shoes, shoe repair
Foodstuffs and consumables	Grocery, butchers and poultry, bakery, fishmongers, greengrocers, confectionery, health foods, organic foods, delicatessen
Furniture and carpets	Curtains, sofas, soft furnishings
Garden products	Flowers, plants, gardening equipment
Hairdressing	Beauty treatments and associated products
Household and textiles	China, household linens, pictures and frames, lighting, drapers, glassware, bedding
Jewellery	Exclusive jewellery, fashion jewellery, clocks and watches
Opticians	Glasses, sunglasses, eye tests, associated products
Pet foods	Foodstuffs and related products
Photographic equipment	Camera equipment, video recorders, photographic services and accessories, printing
Motor accessories	Parts and garage services
Music and video	Records, DVDs, CDs, musical instruments
Rentals	Television, videos, games
Sports equipment	Camping goods and outdoor, leisure goods, bicycles and cycle accessories
Restaurants and take-away food	Traditional foods, international foods, snacks
Toys	Hobbies, kits, games

(Source: adapted from Hemming Information Services, 2006, p. 585)

Retailers also need to consider logistics and distribution: how products get to the point where they are sold (and in the case of online retailing how products get to the final customer). Physical goods such as cans of beans and tins of paint are produced in bulk at one location and are sold in reduced quantities at another. Consequently, the act of breaking bulk and shifting goods from the point of manufacture to the point of purchase is a coordinated activity that is critically important to the success of a retail organisation selling physical goods. Indeed, Walmart (US global retail corporation) attributes its global success to its systems that facilitate the distribution of its products. These systems track the whereabouts, prices and status of millions of individual items every day, which means that within, say, a two-hour window of time, distribution centres can arrange replacement items to be sent to the relevant store, with the aim of avoiding items being out of stock, which means they sell more products and satisfy more customers.

Logistics and distribution is an important issue and is covered in detail in Block 4.

Services

Products and services are closely linked. Retailers sell tangible goods (that we can touch and feel – mobile phones, fresh fruit, shoes, etc.) and add services to enhance the offer to the customer. However, certain types of products are mainly intangible (ones that we cannot carry home – such as a holiday, a haircut, a bank account) and these are called *service products*.

Now read 'Differentiating goods from services', which links to 'The Retail sector' theme.

 Retail sectors ————————————————————————————————

Differentiating goods from services

Retailing is about understanding customer needs and creating and delivering customer value. Retailers achieve this by selling goods and services. Services are special kinds of 'products' that do not necessarily result in ownership; nevertheless, services may be linked to a physical good, for example a maintenance contract (service) for a washing machine (good).

Service products

According to Lovelock and Wright (1999), a *service* is an act or performance that creates benefits, advantages or gains for the customer. The processes involved in the service may be tied to physical goods but the performance is essentially intangible and does not normally result in the customer taking ownership of any elements of the production process. For example, when you go to a restaurant, you eat the food and enjoy the performance provided by the chef and the restaurant staff but you do not take home the tables, chairs or cutlery you have used while eating your meal. Another characteristic of service is *variability*. It is difficult to ensure that service is the same in every encounter; the individuals delivering the service are unlikely to *perform* in exactly the same way. Some retailers invest heavily in training to maintain service standards.

The difference between goods and services can be understood by making a distinction between the tangible and intangible elements, which make up the offer. If you cannot separate the process of production and consumption then the offer is a service. For example, a restaurant meal is produced and consumed in the same place, whereas a ready meal is likely to be produced many miles from the supermarket where it is purchased – and still further from the home where it is consumed. We call this characteristic of service *inseparability*.

There is one more service characteristic to consider: *perishability*. If a retailer sells pure goods, they can often be stored until they are required for sale. Services cannot be stored into the future. Our restaurateur cannot save empty seats at tables from a quiet Monday evening to sell on a busy Saturday evening. It is very important for service retailers to match supply and demand.

With the characteristics of a service in mind it becomes easier to tease out different offers and place them on a goods–service scale, the position of the offer on the scale being determined by the extent to which there is a services element attached to it, as shown in Figure 2.1.

At one end of the scale are pure goods: those products that do not normally have any form of service attached – such as when you buy items of clothing.

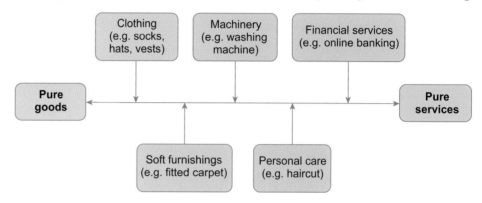

Figure 2.1 The goods–services scale

However, when you buy a carpet, you might want it to be laid for you and for this you may prefer professional carpet-fitting services. Therefore this would appear further along the scale. When you buy a washing machine this purchase may involve service elements like installation and ongoing maintenance, so this kind of offer appears closer to the services end of the scale. At the other end of the scale are pure services. Financial products are largely intangible, as are personal care products (e.g. a haircut), which you experience and see but you cannot hold in the same way you can a woolly hat.

Activity 2.2 Customer service experience

Spend about 10 minutes on this activity.

Purpose: to help you think about your service encounters.

Task: Make a list of any expectations you might have before a visit to the barber's or hairdresser's.

Feedback

Retail services consist of various elements, which largely make up our expectations. The elements include: the willingness of the staff to help you before, during and after the haircut; the ability and skill of the staff to perform the haircut as promised; the politeness and friendliness of staff; the cleanliness of the surroundings and the availability of suitable equipment to perform the haircut; the opportunity to enjoy the haircut whilst being free from danger and risk; and an understanding of your needs and requirements.

To be successful, retailers should list the criteria customers use to evaluate service encounters. For example, a health spa selling beauty treatments will require beauticians with the technical skills to ensure the service provided is consistent and dependable, and the communication skills to talk with clients in an effective and pleasant manner.

Retailers should differentiate between the pure goods element and any service element of their offer if they are to create and deliver customer value. Each type of product has different management implications. Selling service products presents retailers with potential problems:

- the quality of the performance
- matching the service product to customer expectations.

Parasuraman et al. (1985 and 1990) found that matching customer expectations of a service with their actual experiences of a service is key to delivering customer value and ultimately satisfaction. They also found that in order to deliver customer value when selling service products there should be no *gaps* between the customer's expectations and their actual experiences (it is important to note that these principles also apply to the services that retailers bundle with pure goods, such as in-store customer services). Therefore, if a retailer selling *service products* wishes to match customer expectations and experiences, according to Parasuraman et al. (1990) they should aim to ensure:

- There is not a *knowledge gap*: this gap is the difference between what the retailer *thinks* the customer expects and the customer's *actual* needs and expectations. For example, the shift from city-centre, single-screen cinemas to out-of-town multiplex cinemas resulted from research into customer needs and expectations. It was found that the decline of city cinemas was partly due to lack of choice, comfortable seating and parking. Cinema operators developed the multiplex cinema with many screens to improve choice, large comfortable seats designed to ensure patrons could sit through an entire film and ample available parking (Kim and Maugbourne, 2004).

- There is not a *standards gap*: this is the difference between the service quality expected and the operational standards the retailer achieves in its organisation. According to Varley and Rafiq (2004), commitment at the highest levels of management and the acceptance of possible increases in costs in order to achieve higher quality service (e.g. training schemes to incentivise good service) are all part of the process. It is essential for those within the retail organisation who devise service delivery standards and procedures to address any standards gaps identified by customer research.

- There is not a *delivery gap*: this is the difference between what the retailer promises to deliver and what it actually delivers. For example, Amazon the online retailer makes certain promises about the amount of time customers have to wait for their purchases to arrive and customers can choose the speed and cost of the delivery of their purchases.

- There is not a *communication gap*: this is the difference between what the company states it will achieve in its marketing literature and the level of service the customer actually receives. For example, Specsavers is the UK's largest optical retailer and it makes claims about the service offered by using marketing communication messages. One of the advertising slogans used by Specsavers is a claim to be 'Number One Choice For Eye Tests' and 'Number One Choice For Contact Lenses'. From the customers' viewpoint, Specsavers was voted as the most trusted optician for the eighth consecutive year in 2009, which suggests the company lives up to its marketing literature.

By considering the relationship between goods and services you should now be able to understand the differences between them, discuss the meaning of the term service encounter and start to be able to consider the retail management implications of selling services.

———————————————————————— End of theme

Furthermore, for retailers to create and deliver customer value through customer services and service products, they should not only understand customer requirements, but also be able to match customer expectations to experiences. You will learn more about customer service in Block 2 and The Retail Sector theme which runs throughout this module.

Stores

Example of visual merchandising display unit

Retailing activities focus on the *place* where products are sold. In broad terms this can be in a shop or store or via home shopping methods, for example a catalogue or via the internet. Retailers develop their outlets to meet their operational requirements, suit the needs of the customer and create value.

Visual merchandising and store layouts are also important. Retail managers plan where products are placed, consider the type of fitting used to display items and manage the quality of the goods available for sale. Visual merchandising and store layouts are discussed in detail in Block 2.

The place the retailer sells from affects the choice of products, the manner in which the products are displayed and the extent of customer service. Each retailer selects what is important to their customers and designs its outlets accordingly.

Jeff Bezos set out to create customer value by making Amazon.com the world's largest bookseller. This meant offering the widest possible choice of books to as many customers as possible. He was able to achieve his aim, as there are no limits to the number of products that can be displayed through a website but this is not the case for retailers presenting their products in the physical world.

Activity 2.3 How retailers deliver customer value

Spend about 30 minutes on this activity.

Purpose: to explore how retailers use their *outlets* to create and deliver customer value.

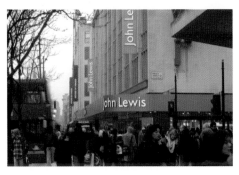

Task: Study the four images above, which show different types of retail outlet: (Kelly's Butchers, Nike Town, John Lewis and a market stall), along with the information in Table 2.3 below.

Using your knowledge of these different types of retail outlets, suggest how each of these retailers might deliver value to their customers, then summarise your thoughts using Table 2.3.

Remember: *customer value* is determined by the *benefits* we get less the *sacrifices* we have to make.

Table 2.3(a) Delivering customer value

Retailer	Benefits	Sacrifices	Comments on customer value
Kelly's Butchers (independent retailer)			
Nike Town (multiple retailer)			
John Lewis Partnership (department store)			
Market stall (independent retailer)			

Table 2.3(b) Delivering customer value

Retailer	Benefits	Sacrifices	Comments on customer value
Kelly's Butchers (independent retailer)	Relationship Product Service	Monetary costs Time and energy costs	Personal customer relationships, specialised quality product ranges countered by higher prices, time and energy required to go to the store.
Nike Town (multiple retailer)	Image Product	Monetary costs Psychological costs Time and energy costs	Image benefits from buying branded goods, extensive product ranges countered by high prices for branded clothing and footwear, psychological costs of not making the right decision, time and energy required to go to the store.
John Lewis Partnership, (department store)	Product Service	Time and energy costs	Wide product choice, helpful store assistants countered by time and energy required to go to the store.
Market stall (independent retailer)	Product Service	Time and energy costs	Specialised product ranges countered by higher prices, time and energy

The type of outlet influences the range of products a retailer can sell. Kelly's Butchers is a small store, which means there will be limits on the range of products available for sale; similar space restrictions apply to the market stall. However, both of these retailers are likely to specialise and so can offer a good selection of products within a narrow range. In contrast, the John Lewis Partnership (JLP) department store sells a diverse range of products – e.g. clothing, furniture, beauty products, textiles – but might not offer the same level of choice in each range as specialist retailers. The Nike Town store has extensive space to display products and emphasise the benefits of buying into the brand.

Remember that benefits and sacrifices are based on personal perceptions of reality and therefore they can differ significantly.

In this section, we have looked at the definition of retailing and its links to understanding, creating and delivering customer value. In the final part of this session, we are going to look at how retailing changes over a period.

2.4 Development of retailing

As consumers, our needs change and this can affect trading conditions. The 2008/09 'credit crunch' has affected our spending patterns and, whilst retailers can adapt product ranges to meet our needs and changing economic circumstances fairly rapidly, the way their companies are organised and the stores they operate from change over a longer period. According to Varley and Rafiq (2004, p. 35), the ways in which retailers evolve have been the subject of academic debate for over half a century and there are several theories that attempt to explain patterns of retail development. We are now going to look at three of these theories: the accordion theory, the wheel of retailing and the retail life-cycle.

The accordion theory

The accordion theory (also known as the generalist–specialist tendency) (Hollander, 1966) focuses on how the retail industry tends to alternate between periods of growth in specialist retailers that offer narrow product assortments, and periods of growth in generalist retailers that sell a greater variety of products.

According to McGoldrick, this theory is best applied in the USA. He states:

> In early settlements, the general store stocked a very diverse range, but as settlements grew and developed, so did more specialized stores. Department stores subsequently emerged, offering wide assortments, but these then lost ground to more specialised chains. From the 1950's many of the specialists started to proliferate their product ranges, notably the supermarkets and drug stores. The term 'scrambled merchandising' described the practice of selling product lines not traditional in this type of outlet. This form of merchandising sought to satisfy the demand for one-stop shopping. However, as consumers became more demanding of choice, some of the more specialist stores proved best able to meet the demand for choice in depth.
>
> (McGoldrick, 2002, p. 157)

McGoldrick (2002) continued by explaining that the accordion theory is limited in its ability to predict future retail trends in general or explain what is happening in the retail sector in particular. However, the theory does highlight that evolutionary change takes place and that the ideas of diversification (wide ranges offered by generalist retailers) and specialisation (narrow product ranges offered by specialist retailers) have worked in certain trading situations.

Activity 2.4 Generalist–specialist retailers

Spend about 10 minutes on this activity.

Purpose: to identify different types of retailers.

Task: List three retailers which sell a narrow range of products but offer a lot of choice within their product ranges (e.g. Tie Rack, which operates more than 100 specialist shops in the UK, selling many different styles and colours of men's ties and ladies' scarves).

Now add three more retailers which sell a broad range of products, but offer less choice within each product range (e.g. Wilkinsons, which sells toys, games, leisure items, DIY, car products and electrical and office products in limited ranges).

Feedback

My examples are:

Specialist retailers

1   The Body Shop, which sells body and hair care products

2   Waterstone's, the book retailer

3   Claire's, which sells fashion jewellery and accessories

Generalist retailers

1   House of Fraser, department store retailer

2   John Lewis Partnership, department store retailer

3   Marks & Spencer, variety store retailer

The wheel of retailing

The wheel of retailing, like the accordion theory, is cyclical. According to Varley and Rafiq (2004, p. 36), 'the decline in popularity of an established retail format is triggered by entry into the retail market by an innovative method of retailing'. Hollander (1960) originally presented the wheel of retailing as a theory that suggests retailing evolves when:

> … new types of retailers usually enter the market as low-status, low-margin, low-priced operators. Gradually they acquire more elaborate establishments and facilities, with both increased investments and higher operating costs. Finally, they mature as higher-cost, higher-priced merchants, vulnerable to newer types, who in turn, go through the same pattern.
>
> (Hollander, 1960, p. 38)

Figure 2.2 illustrates the phases in the wheel of retailing. McGoldrick's (2002, p. 20) suggestion that department stores emerge, subsequently grow and then decline follows the theory fairly well. These types of stores, having begun as low-cost competitors to smaller retailers, improved and developed their offer only to be undercut by supermarkets and then discount warehouses.

Brown (1990) questions the usefulness of the wheel of retailing, but cites Dickinson (1988) to demonstrate its value. Dickinson states that the important lessons to learn from the wheel of retailing are as follows:

1   High prices provide an 'umbrella' under which discounters can flourish.

2   Management must be eternally vigilant on costs, as failure to do so can destroy competitive advantage.

3   New and unexpected forms of competition will inevitably arise and prove difficult to respond to.

4   Success in retailing is ephemeral and contains the seeds of eventual failure.

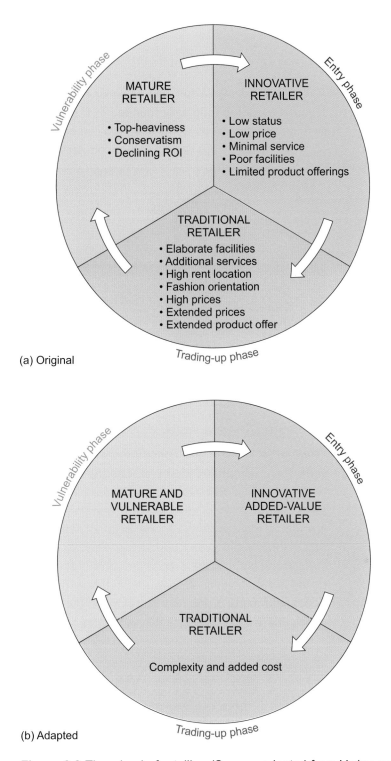

(a) Original

(b) Adapted

Figure 2.2 The wheel of retailing (Source: adapted from Varley and Rafiq, 2004, p. 37)

The rise and fall of F.W. Woolworth & Co Ltd

F.W. Woolworth & Co Ltd was established by Frank Woolworth in Liverpool in 1909 (originally founded in the USA) and the company entered the market as a low-cost, low-priced operator. His stores proved to be a great success selling low-priced items at 3 pence and 6 pence.

A Woolworths window display in 1931

Woolworths profited and opened more stores. By the early 1930s there were in excess of 400 stores around the UK. Arguably, Woolworths had become well established and had moved into the trading-up phase – shifting from an *innovative* to a *traditional* retailer. Trade largely stood still during the 1940s due to the Second World War, but by the early 1960s there were over 1,000 stores. Product ranges had expanded significantly as had the size of the stores, and pricing structures had changed significantly. Woolworths extended into selling more expensive goods and many of the new stores were purpose built. The image below shows the typical (and distinctive) façade of a Woolworths store.

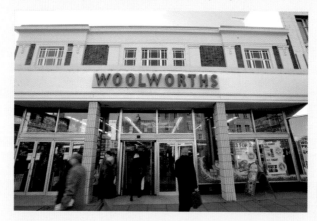

Woolworths in the 1980s

By the 1980s many stores had been modernised and refurbished, the management rationalised product lines, and the main categories became entertainment, home, kids (toys and clothing) and confectionery. However, many major city-centre stores (with multiple floors) were being downsized as operating costs rose and profits fell. The management realised the chain had become vulnerable to new market entrants and as a result attempted to contain costs and began to experiment with new types of outlets. They even opened some new large stores under the brand name Big W, but by 2004 they let many of the stores go to retail competitors. It was probably already too late ('the seeds of eventual failure' (Dickinson, 1988) were starting to flourish). Woolworths had become a mature retailer and was getting weaker, enabling competitors like Wilkinsons (which was rapidly expanding and becoming a major high street retailer) to grow stronger. Another factor which contributed to Woolworths' demise was free downloading of music via the internet. This seriously affected the music business in general and was a significant blow for music retailers including Woolworths. By 2008, retailers were all facing unstable economic conditions.

Finch (2008, p. 1) reported that 'Woolworths is likely to get just £1 for its loss-making 800 store chain' and on 19 January 2009, the Woolworths Group announced it would go into administration, as it could no longer pay its debts. The evolution of this store chain came to an abrupt end following its long, steady growth from market entry as a low-cost innovator and through a very successful trading-up phase. If the management had heeded the warning signs predicted by Dickinson's analysis of the wheel of retailing, could they have taken actions earlier that would have saved the chain? Probably not.

So what does this mean for the wheel of retailing theory? Varley and Rafiq state that:

> While the wheel theory can be illustrated by the evolution of a number of types of retail organizations … such as department stores, supermarkets and factory outlets, it is increasingly difficult to apply because of the assumption that innovative retailers operate on a low-price, low-status minimalist basis. Recent innovations such as internet retailing and forecourt retailing offer added value to consumers in ways that are convenience, rather than price driven. Nevertheless, the wheel concept should alert retail managers who depend on one particular retail format to the dangers of vulnerability in the face of indirect competition from innovative retailers.

> (Varley and Rafiq, 2004, p. 38)

The retail life-cycle

Davidson et al. (1976) attempted to overcome the problems of the wheel of retailing by introducing the retail life-cycle.

The retail life-cycle suggests that there is an introduction phase for a new type of retail operation, a growth stage where sales are growing rapidly but profits are low, a maturity stage where competitors grow stronger, and a decline stage. The application of this theory highlights how retail life-cycles are shortening, and this is important for retail planners.

Each of these cyclical theories has contributed something to our understanding of how retailing develops over time, but they also suffer from the weaknesses of being inflexible and focusing on patterns rather than processes (McGoldrick, 2002).

Other major factors that affect retail development are political and legal, economic, social, technological and environmental trends. The next two sessions examine how the trading environment affects retail development.

2.5 Conclusions

In this study session we have discussed the definition of retailing and explored the importance of the concept of customer value to retailers. We looked at how retailers create and deliver customer value through products and stores. We considered how to differentiate between goods and services in our exploration of the 'The Retail Sector' theme. In the final section, you have studied the theories which seek to explain the evolution of retailing. We hope this study session has helped you to develop your understanding of retailing and helped you shape your opinions about the practices of modern retailers.

In the next study session, you will learn how the trading environment impacts on retail management practices.

Learning outcomes

When you have completed all the study elements for this session, you should be able to:

- explain the difference between goods and services and identify the implications for retail management
- discuss the changes taking place in retailing and offer explanations for the underlying reasons for such changes
- draw on and apply retail theories to help solve management problems and issues
- use your own experiences to learn about retail management.

You should also have developed your learning by completing the activities and reflections in this study session.

Session 3 Understanding the retail environment (Part 1)

Why are we studying the retail environment? Modern retailers face many challenges from within and outside the business and have to understand many things: not only how to operate a store at maximum efficiency levels, the needs and wants of their customers and why and how they shop, but also the business environment in which retailing takes place.

The business environment has a number of elements that can affect the way the business operates. Figure 3.1 shows the elements which make up the retail environment.

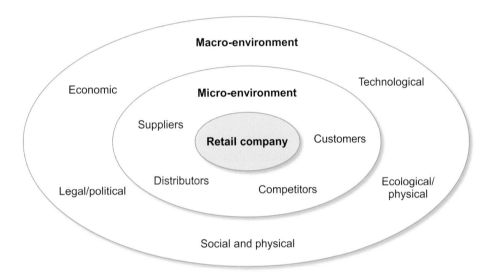

Figure 3.1 The retail environment

> The marketing environment consists of the actors and forces that affect a company's capability to operate effectively in providing products and services to its customers... It is useful to classify these forces into the macro-environment and the microenvironment. The macro-environment consists of a number of broad forces that affect not only the company but also the other actors in the microenvironment.
>
> (Jobber, 2010, p. 73).

The business environment is constantly evolving to reflect fundamental long-term changes taking place in the world of business. Recently, *ecological and physical forces* have been added to the model, reflecting the growing importance of these forces on companies. Customer demand is encouraging businesses to find ways to reduce their carbon emissions in an attempt to quell climate change.

Let's find out more about these forces, which can shape the retail environment. PEEST is a useful acronym to help you remember the names of each of the forces in the macro-environment and we will use this to structure our exploration of how each force can affect retailing:

- Political (and legal forces)
- Economic forces
- Ecological/physical forces
- Social/cultural forces
- Technological forces.

In this session we are going to explore how political and legal forces, economic forces, and ecological/physical forces shape the environment in which retailers trade.

3.1 Political and legal forces

Political and legal forces can influence retail management decisions by determining rules and responsibilities to which retailers have to adhere. For example; the European Union (EU) urged all member states to ban smoking in public places due to the potential health risks to passive smokers. Now the ban has been implemented across the British Isles (excluding Sark). The implications are that retailers must ensure smoke-free stores for customers and staff to protect people from the associated risks of second-hand (passive) smoking.

Politicians can affect businesses through their power to change laws and regulations. Many business leaders try to develop relationships with politicians in the hope that they can influence the political decision-making process, and help to ensure that changes do not negatively affect their companies. Most notably, the star of the popular television show and successful business leader, Lord Alan Sugar, walked into Downing Street on 4 June 2009 and was told 'You're hired' by then Prime Minister Gordon Brown (Wooding, 2009). He walked out as the 'Enterprise Tsar'.

According to Jobber (2010, p. 73) 'Never has the relationship between political forces and businesses been more apparent than in the recent "credit crunch", which has forced governments to financially support banks and, in the case of the British Government, acquire Northern Rock.'

European legislation

In Europe, companies are influenced by legislations at EU level and at national level. For retailers, competition legislation is of major importance and is based on the principles that businesses benefit from operating in intensely competitive trading environments.

The role of competition policy is to encourage competition in the EU by removing restrictive practices and other anti-competitive activities. This is accomplished by tackling barriers to competition through rules that form a legal framework within which EU firms must operate. The legal rules seek to:

- prevent collusion through price fixing, and any collaborative activities that enable companies to join together and act as a monopoly
- prevent companies abusing a position of market dominance
- control growth of companies through acquisitions and mergers, aiming to stop them gaining excessive market power
- restrict state aid – it can be in a nation's interest for its government to give state aid to ailing companies, which could give the company unfair competitive advantage.

(Adapted from Jobber, 2010, p. 74)

National legislation

Each member state of the EU has the right to make its own laws governing business practices. We will now consider two areas of British law that are important for retailers: consumer protection and employee-related legislation. Varley and Rafiq (2004) examine these two areas of law in their book *Principles of Retail Management*. We will take a look at their findings in the following two sections.

Consumer protection

In the UK, consumer protection legislation (supplemented by EU legislation) aims to provide consumers with certain basic rights that can be enforced through the courts if necessary. The Sale of Goods Act 1979, amended by the Sale and Supply of Goods Act 1994 and Sale of Goods Act 1995 specify that buyers have the right to expect that the goods they buy are:

- of satisfactory quality
- fit for all intended purposes and
- as described.

This means that retailers must offer a refund to customers where faulty goods are supplied provided that the retailer is notified in a 'reasonable time' that the goods are not acceptable. Alternatively, customers may choose to accept a replacement or repair of the goods, or a credit note. Retailers may also be liable for any losses incurred as a result of customers using faulty goods. A customer has up to six years to bring proceedings against the retailer (Limitations Act 1980).

Consumers have additional rights when they buy anything by mail order or any other method where they do not meet with the trader directly. Whether shopping via the internet, TV, telephone or from a catalogue or magazine article, the buyer will be protected by The Consumer Protection (Distance Selling) Regulations 2000. In simple terms, the buyer is entitled to expect the retailer to provide:

- clear information about products offered for sale
- the right to cancel an order within seven working days for any reason;
- a full refund if they do not get the goods/services on time.

In the case of selling services, the Supply of Goods and Services Act 1982 details the rights of purchasers and the duties of sellers. In addition to the rights provided under the sale of goods legislation, this Act requires that services performed under contract must be performed with reasonable skill and care. Customers are entitled to sue the service provider if there is a breach of contract.

(Adapted from Varley and Rafiq, 2004, pp. 305–6)

Product liability

The Consumer Protection Act 1987 requires that goods supplied must conform to the general safety requirement. Products fail to satisfy the general safety requirement if they are not reasonably safe given all circumstances, including their intended use, storage, usage instructions and safety standards. The Act also requires retailers to publish notices warning consumers of unsafe goods previously supplied by them and provides powers for the suspension of sale and seizure of unsafe goods. Liability under this Act falls mainly on producers, importers and own-brand suppliers, but retailers should maintain good records to avoid problems (Varley and Rafiq, 2004).

Box 3.1 Product recall notices

1 Morrison's Value Seedless Raisins – recall

The following notice has been issued by the retailer:

Morrisons Value Seedless Raisins, 500g, £0.65

Best Before dates: October, November and December 2010

We are taking the precautionary measure of recalling Morrisons Value Seedless Raisins sold with the use by dates above, as a number of the packets may contain small pieces of plastic.

If you have purchased the above product, please do not consume, return the product to your nearest store for a full refund.

NO OTHER MORRISONS PRODUCTS ARE AFFECTED.

We apologise for any inconvenience this may cause and assure customers of our continuing commitment to the highest standard of product safety and quality.

2 Tesco Red Travel Mug – recall

The following notice has been issued by the retailer:

Tesco Red Travel Mug £4.00

Product: Tesco Red Travel Mug

EAN: 5051898645939

Tesco is taking the precautionary measure of recalling the above product.

Customer safety is always our priority and we have identified that product supplied to store does not meet our strict quality and safety standards and there is a potential safety issue.

WHAT SHOULD YOU DO?

Stop using this product

Customers are requested to return it to the Tesco store in which it was purchased where a full refund will be given.

Tesco apologises for any inconvenience this may cause.

3 Waitrose Natural Roasted Peanuts – recall

The following notice has been issued by the retailer:

Important Notice to Customers

Product Recall

Waitrose Natural Roasted Peanuts 250g

Best Before 03 Jul 10

As a precautionary measure we are recalling the above product, as some packs may contain small pieces of rubber.

Any customers who have bought packs with the above date code should not consume them, but return them to Waitrose for a full refund.

No other date codes or products are affected by this recall.

We apologise for any inconvenience to our customers.

(Source: Trading Standards Institute http://www.tradingstandards.gov.uk/advice/advice-recall-list.cfm)

Food safety

The perishable nature of food is a potential hazard to human health resulting from sub-standard food products. There is extensive legislation covering all aspects of food retailing including preparation, storage and labelling of merchandise. There are four key pieces of legislation that all food businesses in the UK must be aware of, namely the Food Safety Act 1990, Food Safety (General Food Hygiene) Regulations 1995, Food Safety (Temperature Control) Regulations 1995, and the Food Premises (Registration) Regulations 1991.

The Food Safety Act 1990 makes it an offence to render food injurious to health and prohibits the sale of food that is unfit for human consumption. It also makes it an offence to sell food that is not what the customer is entitled to expect in terms of content and quality. At the same time, the Act prohibits the presentation of food that is false or misleading through advertising or labelling. It also controls the types of claims made for food. For pre-packed food, ingredients must be listed in order by weight and display the name or address of the packer or labeller.

(Varley and Rafiq, 2004, pp. 306–7)

Box 3.2 Shelf life

Pre-packed foods also require clear marking of a 'shelf life', the Trading Standards Institute states:

> Most packaged foods (pre-packaged in advance of their sale) are required to be date marked with an indication of the minimum durability of the food. There are three different types of date marking: use by, best before and best before end. Use by dates are used on perishable goods which must not be sold or displayed for sale after their marked date (it is an offence to do so).
>
> Foods with a best before date can be sold after that date provided they are of good quality and fit for consumption.

(http://www.tradingstandards.gov.uk/advice/advice-business-fdlabelsum8.cfm)

Other food-related issues covered by legislation include: labelling that enables consumers to make informed choices regarding the products that they buy, for example genetically modified (GM) foods; and food handling and storage. The enforcement of regulations on food safety is primarily the responsibility of local authority officers (in the UK), for example Environmental Health Officers and Trading Standards Officers.

Displaying prices and the law

Box 3.3 Product pricing

Prices can affect consumer purchasing decisions. Products and services made available for sale should be clearly marked. The Trading Standards Institute states:

> Goods and services should be clearly priced. A trader is entitled to decide the price to be charged for the goods sold and services provided. The buyer cannot insist that a trader sells anything at the marked price, whether or not the trader has made a mistake. However, action can be taken against the trader for giving a misleading price indication. A number of unfair pricing practices are banned.

http://www.tradingstandards.gov.uk/advice/problemswithgoods-sum3.cfm

The Prices Act 1974 is the primary legislation controlling the display of prices and it requires the display of the selling price of most goods and the display of unit prices. As Varley and Rafiq (2004) state, prices must be displayed by at least one of the following:

- a price ticket on each individual item
- a nearby shelf-edge label
- a nearby price list.

There are many orders which come under the Act to which retailers must adhere, such as the Price Marking Order 2004, which requires the following:

- Unit prices must be displayed:

  If goods are sold loose (not prepacked) from a quantity on display, for example, the price per kilogram (kg) must be given for fruit and vegetables.

  If prepacked goods are of the same type but with varying quantity, for example prepacked chunks of cheese of varying weight, the price per kilogram (kg) must be given as well as the selling price.

  If the retail outlet has an internal retail sales floor area of more than 280 square metres, the product quantity must be marked (mainly foodstuffs and cosmetics).

  If the product is made up in a legally prescribed quantity (for example bread as prescribed by the Weights and Measures Act 1985).

- All prices must include VAT (except in the case where sales are mainly or exclusively to business customers). Delivery and other charges payable before the goods can be obtained must either be included in the price or be displayed separately with equal prominence.

- During sales and promotions, price reductions may be shown by way of a notice – provided that the reduction applies to all goods, or if not, clearly identifies which goods it applies to. If the same price does not apply to all methods of payment (for example credit cards or cash) the circumstances when the price does not apply and the difference, either cash or percentage, from the marked price must be displayed clearly and prominently at all payment points and at all public entrances to the premises.

(Varley and Rafiq, 2004, pp. 308–9)

Activity 3.1 Are your labels legal?

Spend about 10–20 minutes on this activity.

Purpose: to check your understanding of the legislation affecting the labelling of goods.

Task: Imagine you have a retail business that sells organic foods and produce at farmers' markets. You have some new items, which need labelling before going on sale. Create accurate labels under the images for each of the following products.

Organic carrots

Jar of honey

Home-baked apple flan

Collection of fresh herbs (marjoram, parsley and thyme)

Feedback

How did you do? Did you remember that loose items should have the price per kilogram; a packaged product should have information about its shelf life; fresh-baked items need a use-by date and collections of items (if they can be sold separately) should have the price of the collection and the price per item? Your labels should have included the following information.

Product _Organic carrots_

Weight _Loose Class 1_
Price _80 pence per kg_

Product _Jar of honey_

Weight _454g_
Price _£2.45_
Best before November 2012

Product _Home-baked apple flan_

Weight _400g_
Price _£2.25 per flan_
Use within 1 day of purchase

Product _Collection of fresh herbs_
(marjoram, parsley and thyme)
Weight _Individual pots_
Price _£1.49 each_

Misleading prices

Issues associated with the display of prices and misleading prices are discussed in more detail in Block 3.

Research by the Office of Fair Trading (OFT) (2000) estimated that consumers suffer losses resulting from defective goods, inadequate redress and poor information of around £8.3 billion a year (this excludes the emotional costs and stress which consumers may suffer). The Consumer Protection and Unfair Trading Regulations 2008 aims to reduce trading barriers within Europe and to improve consumer confidence and ensure consumers are not unfairly treated by businesses.

Regulation of consumer credit

Another important area of consumer protection legislation (in the UK) is the Consumer Credit Act 2006. This Act provides the legal framework to regulate consumer credit and covers most aspects of forms of consumer lending. As with other laws protecting consumers, the main aims are to ensure that borrowers have sufficient, accurate information to enable them to choose the best credit agreement for their purposes, and to inform them of their legal rights (Varley and Rafiq, 2004).

Retailers will require a credit licence if they:

- sell on credit
- hire or lease out goods for more than three months
- lend money
- issue credit cards or trading cheques
- arrange credit for others
- offer hire-purchase terms.

Retailers are not likely to need a licence to accept credit cards or allow customers to pay their bills in four or fewer instalments within a year of the credit agreement.

(Varley and Rafiq, 2004, pp. 310–11)

Activity 3.2 Consumer law you ought to know

Spend about 20 minutes on this activity.

Purpose: to consider the application of the law in the UK.

Task: Read Scenarios 1 and 2 and then attempt the questions which follow them. Read the feedback to find out the legal case for each scenario.

Scenario 1 MP3 player

Your iconic white MP3 player, the possession at the centre of your life, breaks down precisely 366 days from the day you purchased it. The large electronics firm that sold you the MP3 player says that because the one-year guarantee had elapsed, there is nothing they can do to help you. You will just have to buy another one.

(Source: adapted from http://news.bbc.co.uk/1/hi/magazine/8253915.stm)

Is the electronics firm acting legally by telling you your guarantee has ended?

Scenario 2 Dream sofa

You've picked your dream sofa. It's an astoundingly cheap £500, you paid by credit card, and you're very excited. The day of delivery arrives but no sofa materialises. You switch on the news and see that 'Astonishinglycheapsofas'r'us' has gone bust. It turns out £500 was too cheap for a quality sofa. The company had been losing money for months. You ring the company and an angry worker answers the phone and is rather unhelpful. They tell you that you are not going to get your sofa or your money back because everything has gone, the workers have all lost their jobs and the liquidators have taken everything to pay the creditors.

(Source: adapted from http://news.bbc.co.uk/1/hi/magazine/8253915.stm)

You quietly burst into tears. No sofa and your £500 is gone too, or is it?

Feedback

The legal case for Scenario 1 MP3 player

The Sale of Goods Act says that your MP3 player must be fit for purpose, which means in other words that:

'It must be as described. It must be of satisfactory quality, sufficiently durable, free from any defects.'

However, you have to take some responsibility for caring for the product you buy in the way recommended by the manufacturer. Therefore, if you have left you MP3 player in the garden in the rain or in direct sunshine then you will not have much of a case.

However, if you have looked after the player carefully, followed all the instructions and it has still broken it suggests that something may have been wrong from the time you purchased the item.

Legally, this is how the law operates:

- Within a *reasonable period* you have a 'right of rejection' – if the item you have bought breaks down, you can demand a refund. (Note: a *reasonable period* is open to clarification depending on the product and the nature of the fault).
- For the *next six months*, you are entitled to replacement or repair of the goods. It is up to the retailer to prove there was nothing wrong with it if they wish to get out of having to do the work.
- After *another six months*, there is still a duty to replace or repair faulty goods, but the onus is on you, the consumer, to prove that there was something wrong.

Furthermore, the key time span is *six years* as that is how long goods may be covered by the Sale of Goods Act. It all depends on what 'sufficiently durable' means. If a light bulb blows after 13 months, this is not surprising but if a dishwasher breaks in the same time period, this is a different matter.

The government's guidelines say: 'Goods are of satisfactory quality if they reach the standard that a reasonable person would regard as satisfactory, taking into account the price and any description.'

You should be aware that if you go to the washing machine repairer, spend money attempting to diagnose an inherent fault, and find out you have been using it the wrong way, then you are going to be out of pocket.

The key fact: Your relationship in the Sale of Goods Act is with the retailer, not the manufacturer.

(Source: adapted from http://news.bbc.co.uk/1/hi/magazine/8253915.stm)

The legal case for Scenario 2 Dream sofa

Have you lost all round? No, you can get a refund from your credit card provider under Section 75 of the Consumer Credit Act.

Section 75 only works for credit cards and only works when you are paying for items that cost between £100 and £30,000.

'The bank is ... liable' says Espe Fuentes, a lawyer at *Which?*. 'It's as if the credit card company had sold you the sofa.'

The most straightforward claim is in the situation where the furniture firms go bust and you can claim for non-delivery of goods. However, even if you buy an item and it breaks after, say, 13 months, and the shop that sold you it has gone bust, you can still pursue the credit card provider.

The key fact: Even if you only paid for a small part of the price of the goods with your credit card, the provider is still liable. Bear in mind that the Act only applies to single items worth more than £100, not five items of £20.

(Source: adapted from http://news.bbc.co.uk/1/hi/magazine/8253915.stm)

Reflect on the last time you bought an item that was faulty or defective. What did you do – take the item back to where you bought it? Was the retailer able to deal with the situation in a satisfactory manner? Alternatively, did you just throw the item in the back of the wardrobe/garage and make a promise never to buy from that retailer again? How many people did you tell about your experience?

Employee-related legislation

Until recently the major piece of legislation regulating working conditions in retail outlets in the UK was the Shops Act 1950, which laid down controls on shop opening and closing hours and employment conditions for retail staff. However, many of its provisions became dated over time, particularly in relation to Sunday trading. The Deregulation and Contracting Out Act 1994 and the Sunday Trading Act 1994, which allowed Sunday shop opening in England and Wales, gave new employment rights for Sunday working and repealed the Shops Act 1950 (Varley and Rafiq, 2004, p. 313). These and other employee rights are in the Employment Rights Act 2008. The Act protects basic rights covering the limit on working hours, night working, rest time, the length of the working day, and leave. Retailers also have a duty of care under the Health and Safety Act (1974) to ensure as far as is reasonably possible the health, safety and welfare of their employees at work.

Sunday trading

The Sunday Trading Act 1994, which allowed Sunday shop opening in England and Wales, gives shop workers additional employment rights concerning Sunday working (Varley and Rafiq, 2004).

National Minimum Wage (NMW)

As a result of the National Minimum Wage Act (1998), a minimum wage has been in operation in the UK since 1 April 1999 and applies to all types of businesses. Employers are committing an offence if they do not pay their employees at least the current hourly rates laid down under the national minimum wage legislation (Varley and Rafiq, 2004). Whether an individual qualifies for the NMW depends on whether they qualify as a *worker*. A 'worker' has a legal definition and depends on the existence of a contract of employment or a contract to personally perform work or services (contracts may be written, oral or implied). There are exemptions to NMW, such as volunteers, persons living and working as part of a family and Directors of limited companies (unless they have a contract of employment that states otherwise).

Rights for part-time workers

Since 2000, new rights for part-time workers have been in place which are similar to those of their full-time counterparts. The legislation means that part-time workers are entitled to the same hourly pay rates, access to company pension schemes, annual leave and maternity/parental leave on a pro rata basis, contractual sick pay, and access to training.

Retailers must also ensure that their employment, promotion, recruitment and training practices do not discriminate on the basis of race, sex or disability, and there is specific legislation governing each of these areas. Retailers must also ensure that they provide a safe environment for their employees (Varley and Rafiq, 2004). The Disability Discrimination Act (1995) is an important piece of legislation that retailers should be aware of as they need to ensure they make reasonable adjustments in relation to the physical aspects of a job to enable workers and customers to overcome physical barriers.

Planning regulations

Retailers are affected by local and national planning regulations. Current planning legislation for England and Wales is consolidated in the Town and Country Planning Act 1990 (TCPA, 1990), which is the legislation the Government uses to determine land usage in order to achieve a balance between economic activity and the quality of the environment. Planning permission must be sought for new builds and for substantive re-development of existing properties. The focus of planning policies can significantly affect the shape of the built environment. Retailers constantly change formats to accommodate new styles of retailing but the buildings they occupy can restrict them, and planning laws will determine where retailers may develop new stores. Planning legislation sets out where retail development can take place; over recent decades, we have seen the rise of the town centre shopping malls, followed by the development of out-of-town retail parks and retail destinations like Meadow Hall (Sheffield) and the Metro Centre (Gateshead). In the mid-1990s intervention through changes to planning policies overturned this trend and subsequently the amount of retail development taking place in town centres increased and this is still the case.

We have completed our broad review of the areas of the law which affect retailing. Now let's move on and explore how economics and some basic economic principles might affect retailing.

3.2 Economic forces

Economic forces influence the fortunes of all businesses, not just retailers. According to Jobber (2010, p. 76), 'the economic environment can have a critical impact on the success of companies through its effects on supply and demand'. There are four major economic influences which are likely to affect retailers:

1 *Economic growth and unemployment* reflect the general state of national and international economies and company prosperity. The world's economy goes through periods of growth followed by decline, which ultimately influence consumer spending.

2 *Interest rates and exchange rates* are monetary tools that governments use to manage their economies. Interest rates represent the price that borrowers have to pay lenders for the use of their money over a specified period of time. An exchange rate is the price of one currency in terms of another (e.g. an exchange rate of £1 = euro 1.20 means £1 buys €1.20). Fluctuations in exchange rates mean that the prices a consumer pays in one country for a product and/or the money that a supplier in an overseas country receives for selling that product can change.

3 *Central and Eastern Europe* – eight central European countries joined the EU in May 2004 and this has had far-reaching implications for market-driven economies. The EU is a massive, largely deregulated market in which barriers to the free flow of goods, services, capital and people among member states are removed. The aim is the creation of a free market where companies can grow (this aim is supported by EU legislation).

4 *Growth of the 'BRIC' economies* – many well-developed nations have mature economies, which are at best stagnant and at worst subject to recession. China and India have economies that are growing rapidly and consistently. During the 1990s and the 2000s, China's economy has grown at an average annual rate of 9.5 per cent and India's at 6 per cent. Chinese consumers have growing disposable incomes which they are spending on consumer goods. Many retailers are focusing on these growing economies as part of their international growth strategies. Growth in Brazil's and Russia's economies is more recent. No longer a communist state, Russia has many cash-rich consumers who own their homes. Russia has become the fourth biggest consumer of luxury goods after the USA, Japan and China.

Activity 3.3 The effect of exchange rates on spending

Spend about 15 minutes on this activity.

Purpose: to check your understanding of changes in exchange rates on product prices.

Please note this task does not take account of many of the complex issues involved in exchange rates; it merely aims to give you an opportunity to think about the outcome of exchange rate changes on spending.

Task: Imagine you are about to take a trip to Germany and you are thinking about how many euros to take with you. You check the current euro exchange rate and find it is €1.5 to the £1.

1   Assuming there is no commission or other charges, how many euros will you get if you exchange £250 into euros?

2   The last time you took a trip to Germany and exchanged £250 the exchange rate was €1.1 to £1, so you were unable to buy the gifts you wanted to bring back. How many extra euros will you have to spend on the trip you are about to take?

3   In which country are retailers most likely to benefit from the current exchange rate?

Feedback

1   €375

2   €100

3   The retailers in Germany as you are now able to buy the gifts you wanted on your last trip but were unable to buy due to the unfavourable euro/pound exchange rate.

To be successful, retailers must identify which aspects of the economic forces are most important and find a systematic way to monitor activity in the chosen areas and track trends. Additionally, they should be aware that the economic forces can change rapidly with fluctuations in interest and exchange rates and demand for goods and services.

Retail demand

Transaction costs are the costs we incur when getting involved in the exchange process.

Intermediaries are retailers which act as 'middlemen' bringing products produced in bulk by manufacturers to market so that consumers can buy smaller quantities that meet their individual needs.

Retailers create wealth through a process called *exchange*. In practice, retailers aim to make a profit by buying goods in bulk and selling them in smaller quantities to individuals. We are going to explore the economic principles associated with the exchange process. Without retailers, individual consumers would spend much time and money (*transaction costs*) in finding sellers of the products and services they require – and would waste time and money especially if the exchange process did not take place.

Retailers act as *intermediaries* in the supply chain and perform a vital function in modern society. Retailers enable the exchange process to take place between producers and consumers. The skill of the retailer is understanding *demand*, setting prices and competing with other retailers.

The theory of *demand* is not really one theory but a series of ideas and observations that model the behaviour of consumers. Like all theories and models, it simplifies the real world so that we can distinguish between the important and not so important factors that affect consumption decisions. It is, however, a very powerful theory that has stood the test of time through its ability to model and forecast the impact of a changing environment on demand and prices.

For a retailer, one of the basic questions to understand is 'why do people buy the goods I offer for sale?' The answer to this is the basis for many management decisions (the details of which we will address later) including:

Pricing	What price or range of prices should the products be offered at?
Advertising and promotion	Which features of the product encourage consumers to buy them?
Purchasing	Do the input costs allow for profits to be made by the retailer?

So, let us start with a simple example – biscuits. What are the factors that affect demand for biscuits?

Activity 3.4 Demand for biscuits

Spend about 10 minutes on this activity.

Purpose: to explore the basics of *demand*.

Task: Make a list of the different influences that affect your decision to buy a particular packet of biscuits.

Feedback

Your list could contain a huge number of factors. At a basic level, demand for biscuits is made up of two things: the desire to purchase a packet of biscuits (hunger, love of sugar, special occasion, etc.), and the ability to buy (having enough money).

Some of the influences that encourage me to buy biscuits are:

- I like biscuits.
- Biscuits are readily available as there are plenty of shops around that sell biscuits.
- I have enough 'spare' money to treat myself to biscuits.
- I may have guests coming round for a 'cuppa' and biscuits go well with a cup of tea or coffee.
- Biscuits are relatively inexpensive.

Now let us see how these influences relate to demand theory and break this down into the following general categories, as shown in Table 3.1.

Table 3.1 Influences on demand

Price	The actual price of the packet of biscuits is a major determinant of effective demand. Generally (and this is known as the first law of demand), the lower the price the greater the quantity demanded assuming all other factors remain the same.
	However, perceptions of price vary and can affect demand: a price of, say, £1 may appear cheap to someone on a good income but expensive to a person on a low or fixed income. Therefore, price is a relative thing for the consumer and an acceptable price is determined by incomes and by other prices in the market.
Prices of related goods	Related goods come in two varieties – complements and substitutes. For biscuits an effective complement might be tea. If the price of tea rises the effect on the demand for tea would be that less tea was bought. This might also mean fewer biscuits being bought, not just because there is less tea to go with the biscuits but because the price of the tea would have used up more of a person's income and so less would be available for biscuits.
	A substitute for biscuits could be cake. If the price of cake fell, biscuit lovers may switch to the relatively cheaper cake to go with their tea and the result would be fewer biscuit purchases.
Consumer incomes	As we only have a limited amount of money to spend at any one time, this becomes a constraint on our buying behaviour and an important determinant of our decisions. The importance of understanding the changing incomes of consumers is discussed later on, but for now it is enough to realise that our society is made up of consumers with very different levels of income. Incomes are also affected by interest rates, wage rises and the level of employment in the general economy.
	For low-income earners the purchase of biscuits can be seen as a luxury – a rare treat, made possible only by the offer of value brands.
Anticipated price changes	Just imagine if a global shortage of biscuits was announced. It is likely that prices would rise steeply and this would control the supplies of biscuits. Accordingly, if consumers thought that a rise in price might happen in the future they might stockpile biscuits to avoid the impact of higher prices. Conversely, if a fall in price were anticipated consumers would wait until the last minute to buy. This phenomenon can often be seen in the foreign-holiday market where consumers wait until the last minute to book a holiday so that discounts and low prices can be obtained. The problem with trying to predict the future, however, is that predictions may not materialise.
Tastes and preferences	Some people do not like biscuits. Can you imagine that? Others have a 'sweet tooth'. Some buy biscuits as presents for others, especially at celebrations or seasonal events such as birthdays or Christmas. All such influences determine our desire to buy biscuits.
Demographics	Basically, the more people there are, the more they will buy. Studying demographic data via census information can help a retailer to understand the profile of the local population based on age, gender and ethnicity. Additionally, consider the impact of whether say older people, men or women buy more biscuits.

Activity 3.5 Complements and substitutes

Spend about 10 minutes on this activity.

Purpose: to consider complements and substitutes for everyday items.

My friend Vanessa and I meet for coffee on a Saturday and we regularly have digestive biscuits with our beverages. Last Saturday, I decided to have cheese with our digestive biscuits. Next week, I plan to have cakes instead of biscuits as it is Vanessa's birthday.

In economic theory terms, when I make these changes I am adding *complements* to the biscuits by having cheese or *substitutes* for the biscuits when opting for the cake.

Task: Using Table 3.2(a), make a list of three everyday items and then suggest complements and substitutes for each of your items.

Biscuit substitutes

Table 3.2(a) Complements and substitutes

Item	Complement	Substitute

Feedback

Thinking about your own recent purchases (small as well as large items) gives a good indication of the complexity of the choices we make as consumers. For some of my own recent purchases I have listed complements and/or substitutes.

Table 3.2(b) Complements and substitutes

Item	Complement	Substitute	Feedback
Winter pansies	Potting compost Garden pots	Other types of plants Growing my own from seed	All of these are fairly close complements or substitutes. Note how retailers will keep items together to aid our choices.
DVD rental	DVD player Television Takeaway meal	Going to the cinema Basic TV	Clearly I will have no demand for DVD rental unless I own the equipment to play it on. Retailers may wish to make it easier to buy the player so that rentals are boosted.
40 litres of diesel fuel	Car	Public transport Walking Cycling	As with the DVD rental above, the substitutes come with advantages and disadvantages.

Also note that a number of these items are 'leisure and lifestyle' purchases and not necessities and so a valid substitute would be buying nothing at all.

Circumstances like those described above generally relate to a large proportion of purchases of biscuits. However, with any rule or economic 'law', there will be exceptions. The price of a packet of biscuits, for example, when purchased as a present for a much-loved relative on a special occasion will matter a lot to the purchaser since they would want it to be known that the gift is valuable and the amount of money spent represents the level of regard for the recipient. This could mean that the higher the price the greater the quantity sold (when the purchaser is looking for a gift). The same purchaser given the job of buying biscuits for a charity coffee morning might buy the largest possible quantity for a given sum of money (and be encouraged by 'buy one get one free' offers).

One further consideration that influences the consumer's decision is that of transaction costs (mentioned earlier). In addition to the price of a packet of biscuits, the consumer must pay travel costs and give up their time to make the purchase. When this is part of a trip to the supermarket to buy a trolley-full of goods, the additional cost of travel is barely noticed. However, when a special visit is made to buy a packet of biscuits the decision may be made to pay a little more at the local convenience store than to pay to travel to the supermarket, simply to pay a few pence less.

Table 3.3 highlights management issues and decisions which retailers might consider when pricing biscuits.

Table 3.3 Factors affecting the pricing of biscuits

Area of management decision	Issues affecting the decision
Pricing	The retailer will want to sell a range of biscuits across a range of prices but for every packet, a specific price must be found. The price must entice buyers, not be a barrier to them. Sometimes particular 'price points' are used such as 99p or £1.99, underlining the need to see the price not only as the source of revenue but also part of the consumption decision.
	'Buy one get one free' offers are also about price and revenue.
Advertising/promotion	Retailers recognise that price is not the only factor affecting demand and so try to influence and control those factors such as shelf position, advertising, in-store promotions (taster sessions). Biscuit manufacturers may engage in their own national advertising and so retailers can benefit from this too.
Purchasing	Since retailers are interested in profits, the cost to them of a packet of biscuits will be an important factor in deciding price levels. Retailers may choose not to stock items where profit margins[1] are too slim or may compensate for lower profit margins on some items (such as value lines) by setting higher margins on luxury items, especially at seasonal peak times.

[1] At a basic level, profit margin is what is left over from a sale after all the costs associated with the sale have been paid out.

Table 3.3 does not fully explain all the issues retailers need to be aware of or how such choices help retailers to create business advantage. Experience, research of local issues such as competitors, and an awareness of consumer tastes and trends are also needed to aid the decision-making process. Furthermore, store location will influence one-item purchases and impulse buys, whilst store size and range of goods on offer, will encourage consumers to make one shopping trip rather than a series of visits to separate stores.

Price and price sensitivity

In a formal way, demand theory can be illustrated by a diagram of the 'demand curve' (Figure 3.2) – for the more adventurous this can also be described mathematically but we do not need to go that far to understand the fundamental model.

The demand curve helps us to understand the amount of an item consumers are prepared to buy at a particular market price.

This diagram simply illustrates the relationship between price and quantity demanded along the demand curve, showing that the higher the price, the less will be demanded and vice-versa. This holds true provided all of the other factors that could affect demand (incomes, tastes, related prices, etc.) remain constant.

As a model it is very simplistic but does have the advantage of reflecting and predicting pricing behaviour should any of those other factors change.

Figure 3.2 Price sensitivity: the relationship between price and quantity

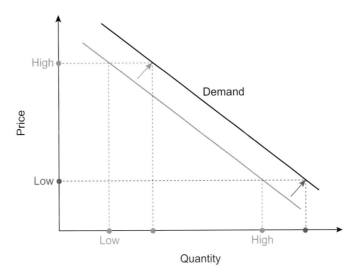

Figure 3.3 Price sensitivity: a shift in the demand curve

Figure 3.3 shows a 'shift' in the demand curve. This means that a factor affecting demand (other than price) has changed. If, for example, the general level of incomes has risen the model predicts that, at all prices, larger quantities of biscuits will be purchased.

In other words, a rise in my household income means that I have more money to spend, so when Vanessa visits me for coffee on a Saturday we can have chocolate biscuits and I might ask other neighbours and friends as well. This means I need more biscuits but that is because I can afford to buy more due to an increase in income.

Another way of seeing this is that if the same quantity is to be purchased then the price should rise.

By multiplying price and quantity, we can work out the total revenue for the retailer. So it can be seen that, provided costs remain constant, a shift upwards of the demand curve will result in higher quantities being purchased and higher revenues and profits being earned. Using this model, a retailer can review the changes in factors affecting demand and estimate how many packets of which types of biscuits to stock.

Activity 3.6 The rise and fall in the demand for biscuits

Spend about 20 minutes on this activity.

Purpose: to help your understanding of how changes in the environment can affect demand.

Task: Using our example of biscuits, list other changes in factors affecting demand that would give rise to a shift upwards of the demand curve. What about a shift downwards? Take particular care to identify price movements in *substitutes* and *complements* accurately.

When you have written your list, sort the changes in factors into fast- and slow-acting factors. For example, a health scare could have a sudden, negative effect on tastes and preferences whilst a rise in general incomes may take more time to work through.

Feedback

A shift upwards could be accounted for by:

(a) a rise in the price of a substitute – such as cake or chocolate bars

(b) a fall in the price of a complement such as tea or coffee

(c) a change in tastes towards biscuits – perhaps following a successful advertising campaign

(d) a news report of a future shortage of biscuits.

A shift downwards could be accounted for by:

(a) a fall in the price of a substitute – such as cake or chocolate bars

(b) a rise in the price of a complement such as tea or coffee

(c) a change in tastes away from biscuits – perhaps following a health scare or report linking biscuits with ill health

(d) a news report of a future price decline of biscuits due to a glut of sugar on the markets.

Note that the changes in factors can be fast or slow acting. In the above list (d) could be fairly fast acting, whilst (a) and (b) and (c) would emerge over time.

Demand elasticity

Inverse relationship is a mathematical term which describes a relation between two variables (e.g. price and quantity) whereby as one variable decreases the other variable in the relationship increases.

The retailer will still need to use expertise and judgement to decide whether changing the price will indeed increase revenue (and profit) based on a review of the ever-changing factors affecting demand. The sensitivity of demand to changes in price becomes a key focus for the retailer. Whilst the demand curve predicts an inverse relationship between price and quantity, consider the following example:

The price of a packet of biscuits rises from £1 to £1.10 (a 10 per cent increase) which may be due to higher manufacturing costs being passed on to the customer or, say, a tax increase. If we assume that 1,000 packets were sold each week at the old price (£1) total revenue of £1,000 would be generated.

The reaction of demand to the price increase could be as shown in Table 3.4.

Table 3.4 Relationship between price and demand – price elasticity

Fall in demand quantity	New demand quantity	New revenue	Comment
0%	1,000	£1,100	Revenue increases, as demand quantity is insensitive to the price rise.
10%	900	£990	Revenue stays roughly the same.
20%	800	£880	Revenue falls as demand quantity is sensitive to the price rise.
40%	600	£660	Revenue falls as demand quantity is very sensitive to the price rise.

Elasticity of demand is a difficult economic term to understand but in consumer spending terms it is an indicator of how the demand for a product changes in response to changing prices.

What is being illustrated in this example is *elasticity of demand* – specifically *price elasticity*. Being able to forecast the size of the fall in quantity will help the retailer to decide whether to pass on the price rise (where revenue rises or is unaffected) or to absorb it (where revenue falls).

For goods that have *elastic* demand (*a sensitivity to price rises*), the retailer can try to affect other factors related to demand to offset the negative impact on their sales revenues. For example, new packaging, a different shelf position or additional advertising could all help to soften the fall in demand forecast by the model and help maintain sales.

Price sensitivity can be measured over time by collecting data on changes in quantity following changes in price. From Table 3.4 you can see that it is the relationship between the proportion or percentage of change in quantity demanded that is important – is it higher or lower than the percentage change in price? Where this information is unavailable, however, retailers might look at the characteristics of the product to judge its price sensitivity.

Table 3.5 shows some factors that affect price sensitivity.

Table 3.5 Factors affecting price sensitivity

Factor	Sensitivity
Tastes/preferences (advertising/branding)	Where a product has a strong brand image (e.g. Coca Cola, Nike trainers), buyers will be less sensitive to price changes.
Addictiveness	Alcohol, tobacco, chocolate, coffee – all are potentially addictive and so can be very insensitive to changes in price. This can explain why taxation duties are often associated with products with an inelastic demand, since the tax revenue will not reduce if the price rises.
Who is paying?	Where travel services are purchased and then claimed as business expenses the traveller will be less sensitive to price changes than if they paid for the travel out of their own pocket.
Purpose of purchase	If the product is bought as a gift or a treat the price paid reflects more than the value of the product and buyers will be less price sensitive.
Substitutes	Where many substitutes exist (e.g. different brands of petrol) buyers will be more price sensitive.
Complements	Where close complements (e.g. computer hardware and software) change price, the price sensitivity is lessened for the complement.
Absolute price level	Items with very small prices (e.g. newspapers, matches) will have less sensitivity to price changes than large ticket items such as houses or cars.
Time frame (long or short run)	Typically, consumers are less sensitive to short-run price changes. If, for example the price of petrol doubles people will still use similar quantities until such time that they can buy a more efficient car or public transport improves.

For a particular type of biscuit, chocolate digestives for example, even without data on price and quantity we can suggest that price elasticity of demand is fairly inelastic (insensitive to price changes) since:

- the overall price level is low
- chocolate and biscuits (sugar) can be addictive
- substitutes exist but buyers often have 'favourite' biscuits and so would not see other types as suitable substitutes.

Activity 3.7 Reflect on your experiences

Spend about 10 minutes on this activity.

Purpose: to develop your understanding of the concept of price sensitivity.

Task: Imagine how items that you purchase would be affected by price rises. Try to think of items that you would buy much less of if the price rose by 20 per cent, 50 per cent or 100 per cent, and items for which you would buy the same quantity.

Feedback

From my recent purchases of leisure items (see Activity 3.5) a 20 per cent rise in price would not alter the quantity of winter pansies purchased but a 100 per cent rise would probably limit the number I bought. The cost represents only a small part of my budget. In the longer term, I might think about growing my own plants from seed if the prices kept high. DVD rental would become less frequent if the price rose (especially if the price rose relative to substitutes).

Items such as fuel for my car, however, would remain at the same quantity purchased in the short run – or until I was able to buy a more efficient car.

In our look at economic forces, we have explained the impact and importance of demand theory and considered how it relates to retailing; we have explored the factors that affect price and examined the concept of price sensitivity.

In the final section of this session, we are going to look at ecological and physical issues.

3.3 Ecological/physical forces

The status of the physical environment has become a global concern and a matter of controversy. Organisations need to be aware of the consequences of how they conduct their business in relation to the environment. At the heart of the argument, environmentalists suggest, is the damage caused to the physical environment by production and consumption. Lynas (2008, p. 261) says the amount of fossil fuels required to process raw materials into foods we can eat and deliver them to the stores where we buy the goods is vastly inefficient compared with the processes used in pre-industrial times – if we measure the calories used in the process. He states: '... far more calories of energy from fossil fuels are put in than we get out as calories of food. We'd do better – if it were possible – just to eat oil directly. For example, it takes 127 calories of fuel to fly each calorie of iceberg lettuce from the United States to the UK.'

Retailers are potentially stuck on a two-horned dilemma: on one horn is the need to generate profits through encouraging consumption of manufactured goods; but on the other is the need to trade in a manner that might combat climate change. Perhaps the obvious solution to this would be to discourage consumption.

Currently, there are five environmental/physical issues which are of concern to retail businesses:

1 Climate change. Concerns about global warming and problems associated with climate change have arisen as a result of a quadrupling of carbon emissions over the last 50 years. More extreme weather conditions, such as hurricanes, storms and floods, reported to be associated with carbon dioxide-induced climate change, are already having a widespread impact on major manufacturing industries, which is filtering down the supply chain. The effect on the business environment is that companies are more aware of ethical trading issues, which has given rise to the concept of corporate social responsibility (CSR). CSR is the principle that an organisation should be responsible and accountable for how it affects society and the physical environment.

2 Pollution control. The manufacture and disposal of products can have a harmful effect on the quality of the physical environment. For example, the great Pacific garbage patch is a mass of marine pollution made up of waste plastic, bottle tops, carrier bags and a plethora of other plastic consumables and other materials that have been picked up by ocean currents and amassed in the Eastern Pacific Ocean. The retail industry is responding and one of the most visible initiatives from the consumer perspective is the reduction in the number of plastic carrier bags.

In response to the news that leading supermarkets and their customers in England are now using 346 million fewer single-use carrier bags every month than in 2006, the then Environment Secretary, Hilary Benn, said:

> This is a great achievement by the seven supermarkets and their customers and it shows that by working together, we really can change our bag habits. The target of a 50 per cent reduction was only narrowly missed and retailers have really put a lot into this in the last six months. This means that several hundred million fewer carrier bags are going to landfill every month and we're using less raw materials to make them, which is great news. I look forward to seeing further reductions in the months ahead.

> Defra and the Waste & Resources Action Programme will continue to work closely with the British Retail Consortium and retailers on further reductions over the next year.

> (Defra, 2009)

This is a voluntary action taken by retailers; in other countries governments have begun to introduce higher taxes as anti-pollution measures.

3 Energy conservation. The finite nature of the world's resources has stimulated a drive towards conservation. Attention focuses on reduction in reliance on fossil fuels. Sweden is aiming to be the world's first oil-free economy by 2020 by using renewable energy sources such as wind, wave and geothermal energy, and waste heat; and Sweden's tax system penalises the use of polluting energy sources such as coal and oil.

For retailers, fuel consumption has implications throughout the business: building design, store operations, distribution systems and product choices.

4 Environmentally friendly ingredients. There is a growing trend to use more biodegradable and natural ingredients. Manufacturers such as Estée Lauder are beginning to launch products like Origins, a range of vegetable-based skincare products. Consumer groups have forced issues about genetically modified foods into media headlines and have encouraged supermarkets in Austria, France, Germany, Greece, Italy and Luxembourg to ban such products.

5 Recycling and non-wasteful packaging. Germany took the lead in recycling packaging when it introduced *Verpackvo*, a law that allows shoppers to return packaging to retailers, and retailers to pass it back to suppliers. Suppliers have to assume responsibility for the packaging and dispose of it in an environmentally friendly manner. The trend of recycling is not only cutting out waste, but it also makes sound commercial sense. Detergent and soap manufacturers have introduced concentrated liquids and refill packs and have made significant savings, which have been passed on to the retailers. Less space is required to store, transport and display such products, and lightweight packaging is helping generate further fuel efficiencies and energy savings.

Retailers need to be aware of the environmental consequences of management decisions. Ecological and physical forces pose opportunities and threats for retailing, and retailers must decide how to not become ensnared by the two-horned dilemma of environmental forces.

3.4 Conclusions

In this study session, we have begun to learn about how the environment affects retailing by studying three of the macro-environmental factors: political and legal forces, economic forces and ecological/physical forces.

We have looked at legislation which provides protection for the consumer and the employee and has implications for retail practices, such as consumer protection, product liability, price display, the Consumer Credit Act 2006 and employee-related legislation. We identified four broad areas of economic influences before studying in detail some basic economic principles enabling you to begin to understand the importance and role of price and demand, price elasticity and sensitivity and how this affects when and the amount of products that are bought and sold.

In the next study session, we are going to explore the remaining two forces in the macro-environment that influence retail practices before considering the actors in the micro-environment and how they relate to retail store operations.

Learning outcomes

When you have completed all the study elements for this session, you should be able to:

- explain how the macro-environmental forces of politics/legislation, economics and the ecological/physical environment might influence retail management decision making

- describe some key characteristics of retail economics: demand and price elasticity

- identify retail theories and concepts that might help to develop a better understanding of management problems and issues

- use your own experiences to learn about retail management.

You should also have developed your learning by completing the activities and reflections in this study session.

Session 4 Understanding the retail environment (Part 2)

In this session we are going to explore the remaining elements of PEEST – how *social and cultural* forces shape the retail environment and the importance of *technology* to the modern retailer. Then we are going to look at the actors in the immediate environment that can affect a company's capabilities to operate. This will link into our final topic, competition.

4.1 Social and cultural forces

There are three elements we are going to consider that come under the heading social and cultural forces:

1 demographics

2 culture

3 consumerism.

Demographics

According to Jobber (2010, p. 86), 'demographic forces concern changes in populations in terms of their size and characteristics'. Studying demographics is very important for retailers because it helps them to understand how demand is likely to change over time and how this might change consumer spending.

Activity 4.1 Changes in consumer spending

Spend about 10 minutes on this activity.

Purpose: to consolidate your understanding of demographics.

Task: From your studies of changing consumer spending in Session 1: Online Activities, list three major areas of demographics that might be of concern to retailers and suggest what effect they could have on retailing.

Feedback

Disposable income is the income that is available to save or spend after you have paid your taxes

1   Age profiles and age distribution affect the demand for products. In Europe, populations are getting older and there is a growth in the number of over-45-year-olds and a slight reduction in younger age groups. Older people tend to have more money to spend, which creates opportunities for retailers to sell more goods. In France, the average disposable income where the head of the household is retired is now higher than the average taken from all households, and people over 60 (approximately 18 per cent of the population) consume more than 22 per cent of all the goods and services produced in France (gross domestic product) (Jobber, 2010, pp. 86–7).

2   Working patterns affect spending patterns, shopping behaviour and the employable workforce. More working women has caused a major shift in

retail trading hours, which have been significantly extended in the last 30 years, and this has created flexible employment opportunities.

3 *Income and expenditure* affect spending power (also linked to age distribution). Rising incomes increase spending but also affect the type of goods people buy. With more money to spend on non-essential items shoppers are more likely to buy fashion goods, lifestyle products and entertainment.

There are two more demographic influences we should consider:

4 *World population growth* is expanding rapidly (see Figure 4.1) but some countries are experiencing greater growth than others. Changing world populations and developing economies can be attractive to retailers wishing to develop internationally. Tesco Plc has recently announced its intention to develop a 'cash and carry' business in India; it entered South Korea through a joint venture with Samsung in 1999; and in Thailand 'Tesco Lotus' has become the country's top retailer service with an excess of 6 million customers every week (Tesco Plc, 2010, http://www.tescoplc. com/plc/about_us/map/).

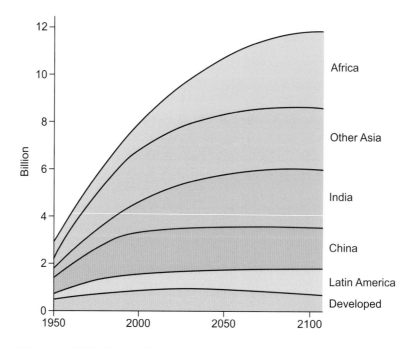

Figure 4.1 World population growth (Source: Jobber, 2010, p. 86)

5 *Household structure.* Changes in household structure and behaviour have significant implications for retailers; for example, in the UK there are more people living alone – either by choice or through marital breakdown. This change alone has implications for the types of products retailers might sell (e.g. a rise in the demand for single portion foods). In Europe, there is a rise in two-income households. This means reduced price sensitivity and an increased capacity to buy luxury goods, such as expensive clothing, furniture and exotic holidays (Jobber, 2010).

Culture

Culture consists of a set of characteristics that identify socially acceptable patterns of behaviour and social relationships within a given social group (or society). Culture sets the rules by which a society operates and applies to all of the members of the given society (Fill, 2009, p. 156). With any given society, sub-cultures can emerge which can be influenced by age, ethnicity and geography. In the UK, there are many sub-cultures which have influenced consumer demand: for example, the movement of Polish communities to the UK means more Polish goods are available from stores and supermarkets. Tesco Plc has created a website (tesco.com/polski) to sell over '250 Polish products, from canned fish and carrot juice to Poland's answer to the Jaffa Cake, the Delicje' (Wallop, 2008). According to Jobber (2010), sub-cultures can span boundaries: there is a youth sub-culture across Europe, which has become associated with particular products and brands such as Coca Cola and Levi jeans. Additionally, this age group has become the 'web generation', turning to the internet for social interaction and purchasing.

Tesco Polski homepage

Consumerism

Consumerism (as opposed to consumption) is organised action against business practices, which are deemed 'not in the interest of the consumer'. This action is taken through the *consumer movement*, which is an organised collection of special interest groups and companies whose objective is to protect the rights of the consumer. Pressure from the consumer movement, environmentalists, the media and individuals who engage in ethical consumption has resulted in many organisations using corporate social responsibility (CSR) to guide their business practices (Jobber, 2010 p.87).

See http://www.mori.com/polls/2003/mori-csr.shtml

Fairtrade now has 18 per cent of the UK roast and ground coffee market and also 4 per cent of the total UK banana market.

Retailers need to consider the potential impact of CSR: if a retailer adopts a *high* standard of ethical behaviour towards customers, employees, the products they buy and the trading environment, the company may be regarded in a positive light. Indeed, according to Besley and Ghantak (2007, pp. 1645–63), there is: 'widespread evidence that customers care about CSR when choosing where to shop. For example MORI finds that 70 per cent of consumers are willing to pay more for a product which they perceive as ethically superior. Fairtrade brands such as Cafedirect command 5 per cent of the UK market for ground coffee.'

Importantly, this study found that 'firms caught out by environmental groups and other campaigners will earn lower profits. In our model, more responsible firms also earn higher profits, as a reputational premium to support good behaviour'.

Retailers should avoid engaging in practices that are considered to harm the interests of consumers, society and the environment.

Currently, key areas where retailers get involved in CSR initiatives are:

- *Environmental protection and sustainability.* Marks & Spencer's Plan A focuses on environmental issues such as climate change, waste, sustainability and fair trading.

- *Community initiatives.* Waitrose's community scheme aims to donate over £2 million to 6,840 local charities and good causes as chosen by its customers and employees.

- *Educational initiatives.* Tesco Plc's initiative enables UK schools and clubs to redeem vouchers from Tesco purchases for a variety of useful items, e.g. ICT equipment, sports equipment and a range of other items.

- *Fundraising initiatives.* Carphone Warehouse set up a foundation to support employees with their own fundraising initiatives. Grants are awarded to charities nominated by employees.

- *Sponsorship programmes.* Topshop, through its NewGen London Fashion Week sponsorship programme, encourages young designers into the fashion business. Designers chosen for the programme receive £100,000 towards the cost of attending the show and creating sample collections. Topshop benefits through spin-off collections, which they can sell.

Now read the two mini-cases: 'Ethics makes good business sense at M&S' and 'Is ethical consumption always ethical?' This is your first encounter with our theme 'Sustainability and ethics in retailing', which runs throughout the module.

 Sustainability and ethics ————————————————————

57

Mini case 4.1 Ethics makes good business sense at M&S

Marks & Spencer set the green agenda for retailers when it launched its five-year eco-programme, known as 'Plan A' (because there is no Plan B). By 2012 M&S aims to:

- become carbon neutral
- send no waste to landfill
- extend sustainable sourcing
- help improve the lives of people in its supply chain
- help customers and employees live a healthier lifestyle.

Progress against these objectives is monitored continually. For example, the company has helped 15,000 children in Uganda receive a better education, it is saving 55,000 tonnes of CO_2 per year, it has recycled 48 million clothes hangers, it is tripling sales of organic food and it has converted over 20 million garments to Fairtrade cotton.

Not only is this ethically worthy, it also makes good business sense. M&S market research has found that British consumers fall into four broad segments:

1 the crusaders (or dark greens) are passionately green and will make every attempt to shop for environmentally friendly goods and services (11 per cent)

2 the light greens want green consumption but want it to be easy (27 per cent)

3 the vaguely concerned are interested in green issues but do not see how they can make a difference (38 per cent)

4 the uninterested do not care about green issues (24 per cent).

In M&S's view these results represent an opportunity: three-quarters of British consumers are interested in green issues to some degree. By taking the lead in green issues, M&S is appealing to the majority of its target market, and benefiting society and the environment: the smart thing to do as well as the right thing to do.

(Source: Jobber, 2010, p. 182)

Mini case 4.2 Is ethical consumption always ethical?

The market for ethical products has proven durable even in the recent economic downturn. Ethical products that appeal to consumers' emotions as well as economic sensibilities have proved particularly popular. Some of the products currently deemed ethical include: fairly traded foods and drinks that guarantee a fair deal to producers in developing countries, organic or local produce, vegetarian products, cruelty-free animal products, recycled and recyclable products, energy-efficient electrical appliances, green energy and rechargeable batteries, eco travel and transport, sweatshop-free fashion, ethical finance and cloth nappies.

Although advocates of ethical consumption believe that we have the political power to influence the marketplace through our individual consumer choices, in practice the extent to which such ethical alternatives are preferable to 'normal' products and services is debatable. For example, some commentators will argue that the premium prices paid for fairly traded goods are not necessarily fully transferred to the farmers under such agreements. Also, although sweatshop working conditions in developing countries are seen as unethical by most western consumers, some will suggest that such workers would otherwise be unemployed. Green claims are also confusing, and it is difficult to determine what the preferable choices are. Organic may be seen as the greener and healthier food option, but many scientific studies cast doubts on such conclusions. Furthermore, recycling and recyclables may seem like they do not negatively affect the environment but, as with all physical activities, recycling consumes energy. Thorough product lifespan analyses in product-specific contexts are necessary for the benefits of green options to be assessed.

Although ethical consumption is important in shaping and maintaining empowered ethical consumer identities and markets, there is much uncertainty about the choices to be made, and at times ethical trade-offs occur (i.e. products are not always organic as well as fair trade). This, in turn, generates much inconsistency with regard to what it is possible to achieve. Although people feel empowered and responsible for environmental issues at an individual level, this is coupled with the insecurity of not knowing what the 'right choices' are, and such contradictions pose huge challenges to policy-makers and marketers alike.

(Source: Jobber, 2010, p. 119)

These two readings have highlighted two important considerations for retail managers:

1   What types of initiatives should a retailer be engaging with to make their businesses more environmentally sustainable?

2 Acting in an ethical and environmentally sustainable manner is a complex and potentially costly process.

These types of considerations have been on the business agenda for the last decade under the umbrella term of Corporate Social Responsibility (CSR). You will be learning more about this topic throughout the module.

————————————————————————— End of theme

4.2 Technological forces

Technologies have always influenced the lives of individuals and the success of industries. Doherty and Ellis-Chadwick (2003, pp. 70–82) state, 'As global competition intensifies, an organization's performance and strategic positioning will become more dependent upon its ability to successfully exploit information technologies.'

The retail industry is known for making widespread use of technology and in doing so has improved profitability, management and control, and many other areas of retail business, for example: distribution and logistics, stock control, staff management, performance measurement.

There are two aspects of technology we are going to explore:

1 technology and the process of retailing

2 remote shopping and online retailing.

Technology and the process of retailing

Customer data is a great source of information and is a key resource that retailers need to manage effectively in order to satisfy their customers' needs and to remain competitive in the industry. The number of products offered by retailers and the large number of customers and suppliers means that retailers generate huge amounts of information (Varley and Rafiq, 2004).

According to Varley and Rafiq (2004), information technology (IT) developments that have been important to the capture and management of data in retailing are as follows:

- *Electronic point-of-sale (EPOS) systems* are cash registers and laser scanners, which you can see at most retail checkouts and cash points. An EPOS system consists of a laser scanner capable of reading a universal product code (the black-and-white stripes or barcode found on most merchandise today), attached to a computer that can recognise the product, with a price look-up table of all products sold in the store.

- *Electronic funds transfer at point of sale (EFTPOS) systems* allow customers to pay with credit or debit cards. An EFTPOS system is basically designed to facilitate cashless payment by customers. An EFTPOS terminal connected to the sales till is connected not only to the

An electronic point of sale

retailer's central computer, but also to the computers of participating high street banks, building societies and credit card companies.

An electronic funds transfer machine

- *Electronic data interchange (EDI)* is the electronic exchange of information between the retailer's computer and that of its supplier. The exchange can consist of orders, delivery notices, invoices, returns and even sales data.

Stockouts means stock not being available for the customer at the time it is required.

- *Quick-response replenishment systems*. When EPOS systems are combined with EDI, retailers are in effect adopting just-in-time replenishment or quick-response (QR) replenishment methods (Figure 4.2). Ordering of merchandise can then be based on real-time sales data. Sales-based ordering systems are now commonplace. This has led to the time between placing an order and its arrival in the store being significantly improved. The speed of response of suppliers can be further improved if retailers agree with their suppliers the level of sales at which orders are automatically placed through automatic reordering systems. A big advantage of QR systems is in reducing stockouts and the amount of inventory carried, hence improving the service to customers and reducing costs to the retailer.

The technology and processes involved in affecting the movement and distribution of stock are covered in detail in Block 4.

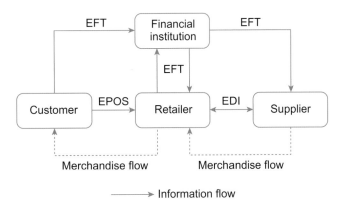

Figure 4.2 A simplified quick-response replenishment system

Retailers have been quick to use these developments in information technology and in doing so have been able to improve the efficiency and effectiveness of their businesses and the quality of the services provided. The use of information technology in retail is widespread and its influence goes into every aspect of retailing, for example: logistics, operations management, marketing, human resource management, financial control, purchasing. Table 4.1 provides a summary of some of the application of IT developments in retailing.

Table 4.1 Application of IT developments in retailing

Area of retailing	Type of technology	Retail applications	Business implications
Store operations	EPOS EFTPOS Bar codes Scanners Self-service point of sale (POS) Electronic self-labels Internet and the web	Product ranges tailored to location Improved customer management Instant price changes Online stores	Increased competition Opportunities to develop customer value Improved pricing strategies Expanded reach to service wider customer base
Marketing	EPOS Internet and the web Electronic displays	Loyalty programmes Marketing research Web marketing Instantaneous pricing	Relationship marketing programmes Targeted online promotional campaigns Improved customer satisfaction
Distribution and logistics	EPOS EFTPOS Bar codes Scanners Radio frequency ID (RFID) Quick-response (QR) replenishment systems	Faster delivery More effective stock management Improved security Improved stock handling and control	Improved customer satisfaction Higher profit margins

Each of the areas of retailing and the types of technology shown in Table 4.1 are covered in more detail in later blocks: store operations in Block 2, marketing in Block 3, distribution and logistics in Block 4.

One other important area of retailing which makes extensive use of technology is strategic management. This is not a topic we explicitly cover in this module; nevertheless it is important to be aware that large retailers make extensive use of retail information systems, expert and decision support systems to improve marketing strategy and planning, and management decision-making systems in order to try to ensure business sustainability and future development programmes.

Remote shopping and online retailing

In the early 1990s, few retailers considered the internet as important to the future of their businesses, but by 2010 many consider it an essential part of their operation's future sustainability. 'Due to high levels of interconnectivity, the Internet is likened to the wheel and the airplane in terms of its ability to affect the future development of business and society' (Jobber, 2010). In the UK, over 90 per cent of businesses have access to the Internet and a similar level of use is found in other countries, for example, Australia, Canada, France, Germany, Italy, Japan, the Republic of Ireland, South Korea, Sweden and the USA.

In the UK, millions of customers now shop online and many retailers have created their own websites to sell to customers in the UK and other parts of the world. For the customer there are many advantages to buying at home (via the internet, catalogue or via the television): purchasing decisions can be made at any time, there are no queues, and you do not have to carry your shopping home as the retailers deliver it to your door. There are some negative aspects to consider – for example, not being able to see the goods prior to purchase, having to return goods that do not meet your needs, potential security risks – plus you cannot see, touch, or feel the item(s) before you buy.

The remote shopping market

The remote shopping market consists of:

- *Online retailing*. This has become one of the fastest growing business sectors. In the United Kingdom, the percentage of online retail sales has continued to rise from £14.5 billion in 2004 (IMRG, 2005) to a total of £20.8 billion (Verdict, 2010). Accounting for over 77 per cent of sales, this type of retailing has come to dominate the home shopping market, previously dominated by catalogue retailing. Online retailing includes pureplay retailers who only sell online, high street retailers with online sales operations and mail order sales. The other remote sales channels account for 23 per cent (£6.2 billion) and include mail order (non-online), agency, direct selling, door-to-door and TV shopping.

- *Catalogue retailing*. First developed by Montgomery Ward (launched in 1872) closely followed by Sears Roebuck (1886), the main driver for this type of retailer was that selling through the post using catalogues meant that retailers could sell to customers in isolated locations in North America. This form of retailing proved popular and by the 1950s Britain had its own mail order houses set up by Littlewoods, Great Universal Stores and Grattan. It currently accounts for just over 20 per cent of sales.

- *TV shopping*. Interactive television (iTV) is in the early stages of development but enables viewers to select a variety of viewing options, and is predicted to become another important technology-enabled home shopping channel. Currently, in the UK, computer ownership is around 70 per cent, television ownership 97 per cent and access to iTV 84 per cent, which shows a significant rate of adoption as this technology only become available in 1999 (Quike, 2009; BARB, 2009). Longstanding widespread ownership and familiarity of television technology could mean this platform might be more widely accepted as a remote shopping channel than the internet, which is still less well understood by certain sectors of the UK population. As a shopping channel, interactive digital broadcasting is predicted to result in iTV becoming not only a source of entertainment but also a highly successful remote shopping platform. Furthermore, environmental influences such as the UK government's initiative to switch off the analogue television signals in 2012, are driving consumer adoption of iTV services. The outcome is likely to be that iTV will be available in at least 97 per cent of UK households and hence consumers will have access to an additional shopping platform. However, at the moment this form of home shopping accounts for a very small percentage of the remote shopping market.

The development and expansion of online retailing

Internet technologies have created a virtual trading environment, 'Cyberspace that can be exploited by commercial organisations' (Doherty et al., 1999), and since 1995 retailers have been experimenting with how to exploit this new environment. Initially, retailers like Tesco and Sainsbury's experimented with selling very limited product ranges such as chocolates and flowers.

Surprisingly, Tesco and Sainsbury's were not the first UK retailers to offer online grocery shopping. On the widest basis nationwide, this was the frozen-food retailer Iceland. Iceland used a carefully planned strategy to educate customers about using the principles of home delivery before launching online shopping via the web on a nationwide basis. By establishing a network of home delivery vans, Iceland was able to solve the logistical problem of how to get the goods the last mile to the customer's home, a problem that was confounding other retailers. In the late 1990s, you could buy frozen foods online from Iceland almost anywhere on the UK mainland. Tesco and Sainsbury's were still exploring delivery options and, whilst they too offered online shopping, these services were restricted to certain postcode areas.

We are now going to take a look at the module theme 'Technology and retailing'. Read the mini case below 'Development of e-retailing' and complete the activity that follows.

Iceland's homepage

 Technology and retailing ——————————————————————

Mini-case 4.3 Development of e-retailing

In the early 1990s, when the development of the Internet as a trading environment began with the first exchanges of commercial e-mail, traditional retailers had little interest in trading online. As this new virtual environment expanded and became more widely known as the 'information superhighway', business communities began to consider the commercial opportunities of trading in a digital environment. However, for many retailers it was considered as a remote 'geekish' environment used solely by computer experts and scientists. It was not until the mid-1990s that larger retail companies began to consider how the Internet might impact on trade in the future and the challenges they might face.

In 1995, few retailers considered the Internet to be important as a channel to market but given the potential of Internet technologies to radically reconfigure the underlying processes of retailing, and because of the highly dynamic and innovative nature of the electronic marketplace, some companies began to test out online trading. Tesco began selling chocolates and flowers, and soon afterwards Sainsbury's and Dixons launched websites. Retailers in well-developed nations, particularly in the US and northern Europe, have spent recent years working out how to best use this new digital phenomenon to support and develop retail trading.

Since 2001 many retailers have accepted the Internet as a durable trading environment and have set about working out how to shape their companies to cope with the demands of trading and interacting in a virtual environment. Difficulties to overcome have been logistics, distribution and how to ensure standards of online customer service. But for companies that have been able to resolve these issues there has been the potential to develop sustained competitive advantages and customer value.

By 2008 most retailers consider it essential to have a website and a growing number also offer their customers the option to shop online. Online retailing has become increasingly popular and important to retailers and consumers around the world. In the UK, during the last ten years, the online shopping spend has increased from around 0.07% to 7% of total annual retail sales. Moreover, recent evidence suggests that consumers' appetite for online shopping is growing rapidly as the Internet has become increasingly accessible, convenient and secure. In the UK, millions of customers now shop online, spending an average of over €800 each in 2006 (Verdict Research, 2007). In the case of Tesco.com, Internet sales have increased to over £1bn annually and profits close to £60m. Tesco offers shoppers throughout the UK a full range of more than ten thousand products online, which can be found in its high street stores, plus a comprehensive and expanding range of non-food goods through the recently established Tesco Direct.

It is interesting to consider, given such levels of online retail success, why all retailers are not following the Tesco model and offering customers similar levels of, say, product choice, service and support online as they do in their offline stores. Sainsbury's, for example, offers online shopping services to around 83% of the UK but there are limits to the product range; Waitrose (in conjunction with Ocado) supply a wide range of products online but shopping delivery services are restricted (by location) to around 40% of the UK population. By contrast, Morrisons do not offer any form of online shopping (Ellis-Chadwick et al., 2007).

This variability in levels of online service and product choice offered by UK grocery retailers (reportedly, some of the most well-developed online shopping services in the world) prompts investigation into the types of formats and operational strategies that retailers adopt when trading online.

E-retail formats and operational strategies

The introduction of online shopping has made classifying retailers by operational formats an increasingly complex task. Traditionally, retailers are classified by: types of retail organization, e.g. multiples, independent, co-operative; format, e.g. store-based, home-based and each of these features of the operation can also be modified by the breadth and depth of product range offered, target markets served and number of outlets operated. Arguably, online shopping formats have evolved as part of the *natural* progression of the retail life-cycle. Davidson et al. (1976) introduced the idea of the retail life-cycle to explain the evolution of forms of retailing over time. Based on the premise that styles of retail operation have a life-cycle in much the same way products do and will start from an *introductory* phase where the operational style is innovative, and then move through into a growth stage as the business expands, into a *maturity* stage where the company begins to see greater profitability and then finally into *decline* stage, where the business is overtaken by more competitors offering different retail styles and operational formats.

In the case of online shopping, the retail life-cycle only gives us part of the picture as it does not take into account environmental influences. Online shopping has emerged in part as a response to the competitive pressures which are the underlying drivers in the retail life-cycle model, and in part due to the rapid development of digital *technology* which has had a profound effect on all businesses, not just retailers, by creating a whole new trading arena. We will now look at *operational categories* and *operational strategies* to build up a picture of the choices that retail marketing strategists face when building and developing an online operation.

Operational categories

To begin to understand the operational styles and strategies of online retailers it is important to consider three main operational categories:

- *Bricks-and-clicks* retailers are generally long-established retailers operating from bricks-and-mortar stores in, say, the high street and then the Internet is integrated into their businesses either strategically or tactically as a marketing tool or a sales channel. According to Dennis et al. (2004) online shoppers prefer shopping at websites operated by established high-street retailers as they understand what a brand means in terms of value and the physical part of the operation gives an increased sense of security.

- *Clicks-and-mortar* retailers tend to be virtual merchants and design their operating format to accommodate consumer demands by trading online supported by a physical distribution infrastructure. Virtual channels have distinct advantages over traditional marketing channels in that they potentially reduce barriers to entry. The location issue, considered to be the key determinant of retail patronage (Finn and Louviere, 1990), is in the physical sense reduced, along with the need for sizeable capital investment in stores. The best-known virtual merchant using this format is Amazon.com, the world's largest online bookstore.

- *Pureplay retailers* – 'clicks-only' or virtual retailers operate entirely online. In reality it is almost impossible for a business to operate online without a point of access to the Internet. Therefore, generally speaking, the term 'pureplay' refers to retailers who do not have fixed-location stores and/or own physical operational support systems, e.g. distribution warehouses. While this category has produced some very innovative retailers, in reality few retailers actually outsource all warehousing, picking, packing, shipping, returns and replenishment requirements. The images below are the homepages of Glassesdirect.co.uk, which is a leading online retailer of glasses and sunglasses, and ebookers.com. Glassesdirect is a company that has redefined the way glasses are sold in the UK by providing customers with a low cost option, whilst ensuring product and service quality that is comparable with visiting a high-street optician. Ebookers is a travel portal that enables travellers to buy a whole range of travel options: flights, hotels, car hire, cruises and travel insurance. Perhaps the key difference between these two companies is that one sells products and the other services. In the case of services, the customer takes themselves to the point of consumption rather than having goods delivered to their door. Other companies which fit this category are those which sell products in digitized form (Dennis et al., 2004).

Glassesdirect homepage

Ebookers homepage

In addition to these three operational categories, there are new types of business which are targeting consumer markets. The growth in importance of intermediaries has led to the use of the term 'reintermediation'. In this case companies, not traditionally service shoppers, use the Internet and the web to connect buyers and sellers through the web and by e-mail. Manufacturers of consumer goods have also seen the opportunities offered by using the Internet as a sales channel to regain some of their power lost to the retailers in the past by the shortening of distribution channels. The process of disintermediation works by the manufacturer excluding the retailer altogether and marketing directly to the customer, thus shortening the value chain and/ or the supply chain by trading electronically and shifting the balance of power closer to the end-consumer. Early examples of disintermediation originated within the banking industry, when it was noticed that information technology and industry regulation had reduced the need for retail banks as intermediaries.

E-retailing operational strategies

The Internet trading environment is largely still in its introduction phase and as a result e-retailing is still evolving. It is possible that virtual merchants (brick-and-clicks, pureplays, intermediaries) could prove to be highly successful, established retailers operating from fixed-location stores but could find themselves increasingly being replaced by new Internet-based retail formats. The implications are considerable, as the provision of online shopping is beginning to fundamentally alter the way that consumers shop, and in doing so revolutionalise the retail environment.

Dutch researchers Weltevreden and Boschma (2007) have developed a typology which categorises potential operational strategies that retailers might adopt and develop into information-based and sales-based strategies (See the Internet operational strategies table).

Information-only strategies (adapted from Weltevreden et al., in Chaffey, 2005)

- Billboards strategy: retailers use this type of website to provide information primarily to make customers aware of the company's existence. The site will not provide specific product information and only gives limited details about services offered.

- Brochure strategy: this type of website acts as a showcase providing information with a little more detail of specific products, say, new product lines.

- Catalogue strategy: this type of website provides detailed product information but offers little in terms of additional services.

- Service strategy: this type of website provides customers with access to a range of support services which can help build and develop customer relationships, e.g. searchable database of customer support information.

Online sales strategies

- Export strategy: in this case retailers sell online but the operation has no linkages to the physical retail presence the retailer may have in the high street. This strategy is sometimes adopted when entering a new market and can limit risk for a well-established brand.

- Mirror strategy: in this case a website has the look and feel of a retailer's offline operation but there are no linkages between the online and offline channel. The website is almost like an additional store.

- Synergy strategy: in this case there are strong links between the online and offline operations, e.g. cross-promotions, returns of goods ordered online can be taken back into the physical store.

- Anti-mirror strategy: here the website has become the dominant sales channel and physical stores are used to support the web operation rather than the other way around.

- Virtual strategy: the retailer either gives up the physical presence or does not develop one. It should be noted in this case the distinction between category and strategy becomes blurred.

Internet operational strategies

Strategy	Product information	Synergies/ additional services	Online sales physical channel(s)	Physical outlets	Website resembles	Physical outlets have limited functions
Billboard	None	None/limited	No	Yes	-	No
Brochure	Limited	None/limited	No	Yes	-	No
Catalogue	Extensive	None/limited	No	Yes	-	No
Service	Limited/ extensive	Extensive	No	Yes	-	No
Export	Extensive	None/limited	Yes	Yes	No similarity	No
Mirror	Extensive	None/limited	Yes	Yes	Strong similarity	No
Synergy	Extensive	Extensive	Yes	Yes	Similarity	No
Anti-mirror	Extensive	None/limited	Yes	Yes	Similarity	Yes
Virtual	Extensive	Limited/ extensive	Yes	No	-	-

Source: Adapted from Table 11.5, Weltevreden et al. in Chaffey (2005)

Perhaps the key question is how do retailers select the right strategy to adopt? There is a pattern of retail adoption, whereby retailers move from information-based strategies to online sales strategies. A five-year study examining the extent of Internet adoption in the UK by Ellis-Chadwick et al. (2002) found that traditional retailers are increasingly likely to begin by having an information-based website and then develop services before offering online sales. European retailers are seen as being advanced in their use of computer-based technologies, so it comes as no surprise that some retail companies were quick to explore the commercial potential of the Internet. But it has taken time for companies to assess and develop a strategic significance for their online activities. Typically, a newly established retail website aims to cover a range of business objectives but is likely to show limited evidence of targeting of content towards specific online consumers; corporate information for investors has often been presented alongside details of consumer promotions and graduate recruitment features. However, as the web usage develops, the focus and strategic contribution of the online channels change.

Retail channel
Retailers' use of the Internet as both a communication and a transactional channel concurrently in business-to-consumer markets

Share of voice
The relative advertising spend of the different competitive brands within the product category. Share of voice is calculated by dividing a particular brand's advertising spend by the total category spend (De Pelsmacker et al., 2004).

As retailers develop their usage of the Internet for providing information, customer services and online sales it becomes a retail channel. This term was introduced by Doherty et al. (1999) to describe companies' multi-purpose adoption of the Internet, using it as both a communication and transactional channel concurrently in business-to-consumer markets. Traditionally the term channel describes the flow of a product from source to end-user. This definition implies a passive, unidirectional system whereby the manufacturer or producer markets through a wholesaler or retailer to the consumer. Recent developments in information technology are changing this orientation by enabling retailers to focus their marketing efforts on managing customers more effectively (Mulhern, 1997). Therefore, the Internet brings the customer even closer to the retailers via a new combined marketing and distribution channel, in effect an interactive retail channel. This move may also suggest a shift towards a bidirectional retailer-consumer relationship, in which more power accrues to the customer. (Hagel and Armstrong, 1997). As a result of the technological capacity e-retailers are becoming increasingly creative with how they are using the Internet and associated digital technologies to serve the needs of their online customers.

(Source: Chaffey et al., 2009, pp. 628–33)

Activity 4.2 Types of e-retailers

Spend 10 minutes on this activity.

Purpose: to learn about the development and different forms of online retailing.

Task: Based on your reading of 'Development of e-retailing', answer the following questions:

1   What are the three operational styles that retailers might choose to use for their online operation?

2   Not all retail websites sell products online. Name two types of 'information strategy'.

3   What does the article suggest is the key question for retailers when they are deciding how to use the web?

Feedback

1   Bricks and clicks, clicks and mortar, pure-play retailers.

2   Any two of the following: billboard, brochure, catalogue, service.

3   How do retailers select the right strategy to adopt?

The reading has raised questions about how retailers choose their online strategies and whether to sell online or not. Additionally, it has enabled you to learn more about the development of online retailing and to consider different approaches to using web technologies for online retailing. You will encounter more discussion of the impact of e-retailing and how technology is used in retailing throughout the module.

This concludes your studies of the macro-environmental forces. The next section focuses on the micro-environment.

 End of theme

4.3 Micro-environment

As we discovered in Session 3, the micro-environment consists of the *actors* in the retailer's immediate environment that can affect business performance.

Who are the groups of actors?

1   *Customers*. As we discovered in Session 2, this group of actors is at the centre of everything a retailer aims to achieve. We have already studied how retailers might develop added value through understanding the needs of the customer. In Block 2, we will be exploring customer service and in Block 3 we will consider consumer behaviour in detail.

2   *Competitors*. In Session 1 we heard about the competitive behaviour of retailers in the book business. The important thing to remember is that competitors can have a major influence on success. Retailers that base their business on delivering added value and satisfying their customers constantly need to monitor the behaviour of their competitors.

3   *Distributors*. Retailers can be classed as distributors as they pass goods from a manufacturer to the end user (the individual customer). According to Jobber (2010, p. 93) 'distributors can reduce the profitability of suppliers by putting pressure on profit margins. For example large retailers such as Walmart and Tesco have enormous buying power and can demand low prices from their suppliers.'

4   *Suppliers*. This group of actors can affect the profits of retailers. Increases in supply costs can push up prices and make alternative products appear more attractive.

Retailers should monitor the behaviour of the actors in the micro-environment in order to identify opportunities and threats that might arise. The next section focuses on retail competition as it explains some of the patterns of retailer development and the shift in power away from the suppliers (manufacturers) towards the retailer.

4.4 Competition in retail markets

There are many economic factors that can affect retailing and the demand for products – and the cost of running retail businesses is affected by the competitive behaviour of other retailers. Some of the reasons retailing is becoming increasingly competitive are as follows:

- *Mature retail markets* (limited or slow growth). Sometimes the only way that retailers can grow is to take sales (market share) away from each other.
- *A new retail channel* (the emergence of the internet). This is raising customer service expectations and enabling competitors, in the form of manufacturers, to enter retail markets.
- *Globalisation*. This means retailers have to react to and defend their market share from domestic and international competitors. Notable examples of retailers expanding out of their domestic market include: Walmart's (USA) acquisition of ASDA; IKEA, the Swedish furniture retailer; and European discounters such as Aldi, Lidl and Netto.

The rest of this section aims to extend your understanding of the dynamics of retail competition by looking at the following:

- measures of retail competition
- types of competition
- strategic groups.

Measures of retail competition

According to Varley and Rafiq (2004), a frequently used measure of the competitiveness of a market is the degree of concentration in the market. One way to measure retail concentration is by calculating the percentage of the total market controlled by the largest four or five retailers in a given sector. It is important to note that the trend in developed countries is for increasing concentration/dominance of the market by a small number of large players. The reason for this is the growth of multiple retailers.

Once a large retail organisation has established a successful retail store, the organisation is able to expand rapidly. In the UK grocery sector the four top retailers account for more than 75 per cent of the market; see Table 4.2.

Table 4.2 Multiple grocers' market share

	12 weeks to 18 May 2008	12 Weeks to 17 May 2009
Tesco	31.1%	30.8%
Asda	16.9%	17.1%
Sainsbury's	16.0%	16.3%
Morrisons	11.4%	11.6%
Somerfield	3.7%	3.2%
Waitrose	3.9%	3.8%
Aldi	2.8%	3.0%
Lidl	2.2%	2.4%
Iceland	1.7%	1.7%
Netto	0.7%	0.7%
Farmfoods	0.5%	0.6%
Other freezer centres	0.2%	0.2%
Other multiples	1.6%	1.8%
Total co-ops	4.3%	4.3%
Total independents	2.8%	2.4%

(Source: IDG Retail Analysis http://www.igd.com/analysis/news/index.asp?nid=5876)

A feature of retail concentration is that it tends to be much higher at the local level than at the national level, which has led to a discussion of local retailing being dominated by one or two very large retailers – this often results in small independent retailers being forced to close.

Whilst the measure of retail competition and market shares are good indicators of intensity of competition, the data is not always available. An alternative measure is the number of retail outlets of a particular type of retailer per thousand of population. The higher the ratio is, the higher the competitive intensity. When the ratio of store to population gets too high, the market is described as *overstored*. This means the size of the population in an area is insufficient for all the stores to operate profitably, leading to intense competition as retailers try to improve sales and profit performance. Conversely, if the ratio of stores to population is relatively small, the market is said to be *understored*. In this situation, there is unsatisfied demand and retailers will enjoy high profits. This leads to existing retailers expanding their operations and other retailers being attracted into the market. Please note that this discussion assumes the retailers are of a similar size. A refinement to this method is to measure the total amount of retail space occupied by a particular type of retailer per thousand of population.

To be successful, retailers must identify the most attractive markets and regions. Regions, towns, cities, and metropolitan conurbations are all potential sites for locating retail stores. A retailer will need to assess a location, considering the demand (from the consumer) and the competition from other retailers before deciding on the type and location of a new store.

The location or trading area is defined as a geographic area from where a store draws its customers. The extent of the store is determined by the type of store, the degree of mobility of the customer and the relative location of the competitors. For instance, the trading area of a convenience store is less than 1 mile, whereas for an IKEA store it may extend to 20 miles.

The difference in the distances is because customers are not willing to travel long distances for convenience items such as bread and milk but will travel further for speciality, comparison and large assortments.

Other influences on the size of the trading area are:

- population density
- socioeconomic status of consumers
- distance and time to travel
- transportation
- level of car ownership
- business attractions
- social attractions
- competition from neighbouring stores/centres
- presence of complementary retailers
- geographical barriers.

The actual shape and size of the trading area will be determined by the interaction of all of these factors. Retail trading areas can be classified as primary, secondary and tertiary:

1 The *primary trade area* is designated as the area from which the store attracts 60–65 per cent of its customers.

2 The *secondary trade area* generates 20–30 per cent of the stores' sales.

3 The *tertiary trade area* accounts for the remaining sales.

There are two main techniques for determining trade areas:

1 *Spotting techniques* are mainly used to determine the extent of trading areas for existing stores. A retailer will seek to identify where customers live and deduce the major concentrations of customers within a given area. Examples of spotting techniques are: customer surveys, loyalty schemes and sales promotion techniques (e.g. competitions).

2 *Mathematical models* are mainly used when deciding on where to open a new store. The most commonly used models are referred to as gravitational or spatial interaction models, which are based on the physical laws of gravity. The aim is to determine the *pull* or *attraction* of possible store locations. Two widely used models are Reilly's law and Huff's probability test.

Activity 4.3 The Huff model

Spend about 15 minutes reading this example.

Purpose: to explore how retailers might use Huff's model to determine new store locations.

Box 4.1 An Illustration using the Huff model

Huff's model aims to predict the trading area of an individual store and proposes that the trading area of a store is determined by its relative attraction compared to similar stores in the area.

Imagine you have a choice of two supermarkets in which to shop. The two stores are different sizes and different distances from your home. A retailer planning to open a new store will investigate how far you are prepared to travel and the type of store that you wish to find at the end of your journey.

The distance and size of the two supermarkets are as follows:

Store	Distance (miles)	Size (square feet)
Supermarket A	3	20,000
Supermarket B	4	40,000

There are various parameters which affect the relative importance of store size and distance, for example, distance has a deterrent effect in the case of a convenience store.

If parameter a = 1 and parameter b = 2, the relative attraction of each of the stores to you can be calculated are follows:

- Attraction of supermarkets A = $20,000/3^2$ = 2,222
- Attraction of supermarket B = $40,000/4^2$ = 2,500

The probability of you visiting supermarket A is:

$$\frac{\text{Attraction of supermarket A}}{\text{Sum of the attraction of all stores in area}} = \frac{2222}{2222 + 2500} = 0.47 \text{ or } 47\%$$

Similarly, the probability of you visiting supermarket B is:

$$\frac{\text{Attraction of supermarket B}}{\text{Sum of the attraction of all stores in area}} = \frac{2500}{2222 + 2500} = 0.53 \text{ or } 53\%$$

Please note that it is not only the trading area that is important, but also the exact location of a store – a few yards either way can make the difference between success and failure. The reason for this is the variation in customer flows, which can vary greatly, for example, customer traffic can be very different on the two sides of the same shopping street.

Adapted from Varley and Rafiq

Types of competition

Measures of concentration are useful for helping us to work out the level of competition between direct competitors but there are other types of competitors in the market place to consider. Figure 4.3 shows types of retail competitors.

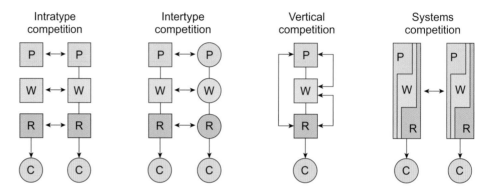

Key: P = producer, W = wholesaler, R = retailer, C = consumer

Figure 4.3 Types of retail competition (Source: based on Lewison and Delozier, 1986, p. 66.)

Intratype competition

This is direct competition between similar types of retailers using similar forms of operation, types of stores and trading styles. The more similar the operations, the more intense the competition and retail managers need to work out how to differentiate their business from others. Carphone Warehouse differentiated itself from other mobile phone retailers by developing a unique position in the market. The company specifically targeted an underserved market: plumbers, builders and electricians.

Intertype competition

This is competition between retailers selling the same type of product. For example, a book retailer like Waterstone's faces competition from other specialist book retailers such as Blackwells but also from variety stores such as WH Smith, supermarkets such as Tesco, and online retailers such as Amazon.com.

Vertical competition

This is competition for different parts of the distribution channel. In other words, wholesalers and producers that sell directly to the consumer. The internet has made this much easier. Probably the most notable example is Dell, the computer manufacturer. Dell streamlined its operations so that it could offer customised computers direct to the end consumer and in doing so cut out several intermediaries (agents, wholesalers and retailers).

Forward integration is the expansion of a business so that it can distribute products directly to the consumer. Backward integration is expansion of a business towards the manufacturer. In other words, buying up the supply chain so it becomes possible to control from the manufacturer to the end consumer.

Corporate systems competition

This is the most complicated form of competition to understand.

Corporate systems are those where the retailer or manufacturer controls everything. In other words, the products are manufactured, distributed and sold by the same company. IKEA is a good example of a corporate system in the furnishing market. What makes this type of competition complicated to understand is how the systems are formed. If a manufacturer develops a distribution system and a network of retail stores, the process is called *forward integration*. There are many examples in the fashion industry: Polo Ralph Lauren, Benetton, Alexon. However, the retailer can also instigate the process and in this case, it is called *backward integration*.

Activity 4.4 Planning how to compete

Spend about 15 minutes on this activity.

Purpose: to identify key considerations for senior retail managers when working out how to deal with competition.

Task: From the discussion of types of competition above make a list of possible sources of competition.

Feedback

Retail managers working out how to compete should consider:

- retailers that sell the same types of products in the same types of stores
- retailers that sell the same product but from different types of stores
- other types of companies, e.g. wholesalers and manufacturers that produce or handle the same type of product
- opportunities to acquire distribution and manufacturing capabilities and threats from manufacturers and distributors that might wish to takeover the retail operation.

The forces of competition act on the companies fighting for a share of a specific market. These forces are based on the interrelationships between all of the players in the industry and the balance of power between these companies (Porter, 1980).

Strategic groups

A group of stores (competing in a similar way) with similar target markets and similar marketing plans is called a strategic group. The aim of the strategic group concept is to help us understand and make predictions about how competing retailers might behave.

Figure 4.4 is a map of competing retailers in the grocery sector. What it shows us is the retailers that cluster together around certain criteria – for example Aldi, Netto and Lidl – are low-price discount retailers that have relatively limited ranges of products of similar quality, whereas the Co-op, Sainsbury's, Tesco and Budgens operate convenience stores that sell limited

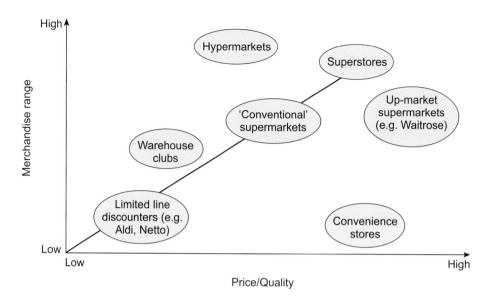

Figure 4.4 Strategic groups in the UK grocery market (Source: Varley and Rafiq, 2004, p. 51)

ranges of products at higher prices. (Specific types of retailers and the styles of stores are discussed in detail in Block 2.)

How do maps of strategic groups help us understand competition? The intensity of the competition depends on how close the groups are to one another. Competition between groups will be more fierce when there is overlap as between supermarkets and hypermarkets. Strategic groupings can be relatively stable but they are constantly evolving due to rivalry and new types of retailing. In fashion retailing, mid-market retailers such as Marks & Spencer have lost market share to specialist clothing retailers, such as Next and Gap and to new discount retailers Matalan, New Look and TK Maxx. Marks & Spencer found it difficult to compete, as its cost-base is too high to compete with the discounters, and its clothing ranges are not sufficiently high-fashion orientated to compete with the specialists.

To deal with the competition from other members of strategic groups, retailers need to aim to stand out. There are a number of different ways a retailer can differentiate its offer in the market place: price, location, product assortments, service quality and marketing communications (these are the principal concepts of retail marketing and are discussed in detail in Block 3).

You were introduced to the theme of sustainability and ethics in retailing in Section 4.1 of this book. The ethics of consumption is of relevance to all of us as consumers and most certainly to many of you studying this module. Please visit your TGFs to share your views with your colleagues on the following question.

TGF activity

Are you an ethical consumer? Discuss this issue with fellow students in your tutor group forum.

4.5 Conclusions

In this book you have learned about the meaning of the potential effects of social and cultural forces on the retail environment and the term retailing. This was followed by discussion of retailer technology and the development and impact of online retailing. Then came a brief review of the actors in the micro-environment before concluding with a look at the potential effects of competition. In Block 2 you will study store operations and how retail stores operate.

Learning outcomes

When you have completed all the study elements for this book, you should be able to:

- explain how social/cultural and technological forces might shape the retail environment
- explain the development of the internet and suggest why some retailers have developed into online retailers
- explain the role of the actors in the micro-environment in shaping the retail environment
- draw on and apply retail theories to help solve management problems and issues
- use your own experiences to learn about retail management.

You should also have developed your learning by completing the activities and reflections in this book.

Block 1 Conclusions

In this block, we set out to learn about the principles of retailing; define the term 'retailing', and explore the impact of the environment on retail management and marketing from theoretical, practitioner and personal perspectives.

You began your studies in this block with Session 1: Online Activities, and in doing so considered some of the practical implications affecting retailing management by interacting with, listening to, and watching a range of online module materials. In this book, you have studied:

- the importance of customer value and customer services and how retailers go about delivering customer value
- the changes taking place in retail and theories that explain patterns of retail development
- the retail environment, by focusing on each of the PEEST factors that affect how retailers operate.

Studying Block 1 and completing the associated activities should have enabled you to develop a good solid grounding of what retailing is about, the major forces that shape the retail environment, and the internal factors that retailers can use to combat competitors.

You should have developed an understanding of retailing which you can use to help you in Block 2 and your studies of retail store operations.

References

BBC (2008) 'Woolworths to close in January', 17 December [online], http://news.bbc.co.uk/1/hi/7787904.stm (Accessed 22 November 2010).

Besley, T. and Ghatak, M. (2007) 'Retailing public goods: the economics of corporate social responsibility', *Journal of Public Economics*, vol. 91, no. 9, pp. 1645–63.

Broadcasters Audience Research Board (BARB) (2009) 'Television ownership in private domestic households 1956–2010 (millions)' [online], http://www.barb.co.uk/facts/tvOwnershipPrivate (Accessed 14 May 2010).

Brown, S. (1990) 'The wheel of retailing: past and future', *Journal of Retailing*, vol. 66, no. 2, pp. 143–50.

Chaffey, D., Ellis-Chadwick, F., Mayer, R. and Johnston, K. (2009) *Internet Marketing: Strategy, Implementation and Practice* (4th edn), Harlow, Financial Times/Prentice Hall.

Davidson, W. R., Bates, A. D. and Bass, S. J. (1976) 'The retail life-cycle', *Harvard Business Review*, vol. 54, no. 6, pp. 89–96.

Defra (2009) 'Millions fewer carrier bags on England's high streets' [online], www.defra.gov.uk/News/2009/090717a.htm (Accessed 28 April 2010).

Dickinson, R. A. (1988) 'Lessons from retailers' prices experiences of the 1950s', in Nevett, T. and Fullerton, R. A. (eds) *Historical Perspective in Marketing: Essays in Honor of Stanley C. Hollander*, Lexington, MA, D.C. Heath, pp. 177–92.

Doherty, N. F., Ellis-Chadwick, F. and Hart, C. A. (1999) 'Cyber retailing in the UK: the potential of the internet as a retail channel', *International Journal of Retail & Distribution Management*, vol. 27, no. 1, pp. 22–36.

Doherty, N. and Ellis-Chadwick, F. (2003) 'E-relationship between retailers' targeting and e-commerce strategies: an empirical analysis', *Internet Research*, vol. 13, no. 3, pp. 170–82.

Ellis-Chadwick, F., Doherty, N. F. and Anastasakis, L. (2007) 'E-strategy in the UK retail grocery sector: a resource-based analysis', *Managing Service Quality*, vol. 17, no. 6, pp. 702–27.

Ellis-Chadwick, F., Doherty, N. F. and Hart, C. A. (2002) 'Signs of change? A longitudinal study of internet adoption in the UK retail sector', *Journal of Retailing and Consumer Services*, vol. 9, no. 2, pp. 71–80.

Fill, C. (2009) *Marketing Communications: Interactivity, Community and Content*, Harlow, Prentice Hall.

Finch, J. (2008) 'Founded 1909, 802 stores, once worth £830m, for sale yesterday for £1; bloodbath on the high street', *Guardian*, 20 November, p. 1.

Hemming Information Services (2006) *The Retail Directory*, London, Hemming Information Services.

Hollander, S. C. (1960) 'The wheel of retailing', *Journal of Marketing*, vol. 24, no. 3, pp. 37–42.

Hollander, S. C. (1966) 'Notes on the retail accordion', *Journal of Retailing*, vol. 42, (summer), pp. 29–40.

IMRG (2005) e-Retail 2005 Annual Report [online], www.imrg.org (Accessed 1 June 2010).

Jobber, D. (2010) *Principles and Practice of Marketing* (6th edn), London, McGraw-Hill.

Kim, W. C. and Maughbourne, R. A. (2004) 'Value innovation: the strategic logic of high growth', *Harvard Business Review*, vol. 82, nos 7/8, pp. 172–80.

Lewison, D. M. and Delozier, W. M. (1986) *Retailing*, (2nd edn), Columbus, OH, Merrill Publishing.

Lovelock, C. and Wright, L. (1999) *Principles of Service Marketing and Management*, Upper Saddle River, NJ, Prentice Hall.

Lynas, M. (2008) *Six Degrees: Our Future on a hotter Planet*, London, Harper Perennial.

McGoldrick, P. (2002) *Retail Marketing* (2nd edn), London, McGraw-Hill.

Office of Fair Trading (OFT) (2008) 'Explanatory memorandum to the consumer protection from unfair trading regulations', No. 1277.

Office of Fair Trading (OFT) (2008) 'The business protection from misleading marketing regulations' [online], http://www.england-legislation.hmso.gov.uk/si/si2008/em/uksiem_20081277_en.pdf no.1276 (Accessed 22 November 2010).

Parasuraman, A., Zeithamal, V. A. and Berry, L. L. (1985) 'A conceptual model of service quality and its implications for future research', *Journal of Marketing*, vol. 49, pp. 41–50.

Parasuraman, A., Zeithamal, V. A. and Berry, L. L. (1990) *Delivering Service Quality: Balancing customer perceptions with expectations*, New York, Free Press.

Porter, M. (1980) *Competitive Advantage*, New York, The Free Press.

Quike, S. (2009) 'PC ownership rises to 70% in UK', *Computer Weekly*, 15 April.

Tesco Plc (2009) Annual Report and Financial Statements 2009 [online], http://www.investis.com/tesco/pdf/repp2009.pdf p. 23. (Accessed 28 April 2010.)

Varley, R. and Rafiq, M. (2004) *Principles of Retail Management*, Basingstoke, Palgrave Macmillan.

Verdict (2008) *UK Remote Shopping 2009*, London, Datamonitor.

Wallop, H. (2008) 'Tesco launch website for homesick Poles', *Telegraph*, 6 May [online], http://www.telegraph.co.uk/news/uknews/1931932/Tesco-launch-website-for-homesick-Polish-immigrants.html (Accessed 28 April 2010).

Watchdog (2009) BBC television programme, 23 February.

Wooding, D. (2009) 'Sir Alan made a Lord', *The Sun*, 5 June, p. 1 [online], http://www.thesun.co.uk/sol/homepage/news/2464477/Sir-Alan-made-Lord-Sugar.html#ixzz0h11PBJlv (Accessed 1 February 2010).

Acknowledgements

Text

Pages 7, 8, 15, 18, 20, 21, 22, 23, 27, 28, 29, 30, 31, 33, 34, 36, 37, 59, 72, 75, 76 and 79: Varley, R. and Rafiq, M. (2003) 'Retail brands', *Principles of Retail Management*, published 2003, Palgrave MacMillan. Reproduced with permission of Palgrave MacMillan.

Page 28: 'Morrisons value seedless raisins – recall', www.tradingstandards.gov.uk, Trading Standards Institute.

Pages 57 and 58: Jobber, D (2010) *Principles and Practice of Marketing*, McGraw-Hill Education, Mcgraw-Hill Education. Copyright © 2010 The McGraw-Hill Companies, Inc. Reproduced with the kind permission of The McGraw-Hill Companies. All rights reserved.

Tables

Table 2.1: Jobber, D (2010) *Principles and Practice of Marketing*, McGraw-Hill Education, Mcgraw-Hill Education. Copyright © 2010 The McGraw-Hill Companies, Inc. Reproduced with the kind permission of The McGraw-Hill Companies. All rights reserved.

Page 69: 'Internet operational strategies'. Chaffey, D., Ellis-Chadwick, F., Mayer, R., Johnston, K., *Internet Marketing: Strategy, Implementation and Practice*, Chapter 11, Business-to-consumer Internet marketing, © Pearson Education Limited, 2000, 2003, 2006, 2009.

Table 4.2: © TNS workpanel.

Illustrations

Cover: Adapted from 3D images supplied by 3DStudio and Turbosquid.

© 2011 Turbosquid.

Copyright © 1996–2011 The 3dstudio.com™, Inc. All rights reserved.

Page 5 left: © Fiona Ellis-Chadwick.

Page 5 right: Tesco superstore, North Berwick. Copyright Tesco 2010.

Page 10: 'Varieties of Indian ready meals', J Sainsbury plc.

Page 16: © Fiona Ellis-Chadwick.

Page 17 top left, bottom left and bottom right: © Fiona Ellis-Chadwick.

Page 17 top right: © Najlah Feanny/Corbis.

Page 22: © Liverpool Daily Post and Echo Syndication.

Module team

The Module Team

Fiona Ellis-Chadwick *(Module Team Chair and author)*
Caroline Emberson *(Author)*
Roshan Boojihawon *(Author)*
Leslie Budd *(Reader in Social Enterprise, OUBS)*
Michael Phillips *(Group Regional Manager, Undergraduate Programme)*
Frances Myers *(Regional Manager)*
Erica Youngman *(Programme Coordinator)*
Colin Stanton *(Curriculum Manager)*
Iris Widdows *(Curriculum Manager)*
Pat McCarthy *(Qualification Manager)*
Val O'Connor *(Module Team Assistant)*
Sue Treacy *(Module Team Assistant)*

Other contributors

Diane Preston, Open University Business School
Mohammed Rafiq, Loughborough University Business School
Keith Pond, Loughborough University Business School
Christopher Moore, Caledonian Business School

Critical Readers

Haider Ali
Kristen Reid
Sue Hughes
Joan Hunt
Sally Booker
Rob Parker
Jerome Kiley
Noreen Siddiqui
Terry Robinson
John Pal
Paul Cowell

External Assessor

Professor Peter Jones, Department of Business, Education and Professional Studies, University of Gloucestershire

Production Team

Jodie Archbold *(Picture Researcher and Rights Clearances Assistant)*
Jill Alger *(Editor)*
Martin Brazier *(Graphic Designer)*
Johanna Breen *(Editorial Media Developer)*
Anne Brown *(Media Assistant)*

Angela Davies (*Media Assistant*)
Vicky Eves (*Graphic Artist*)
Chris French (*Producer for Sound and Vision*)
Sara Hack (*Graphic Artist*)
Lucy Hendy (*Media Assistant*)
Diane Hopwood (*Picture Researcher and Rights Clearances Assistant*)
Chris Hough (*Graphic Designer*)
Lee Johnson (*Media Project Manager*)
Edwina Jones (*Editorial Media Developer*)
Jane Roberts (*Producer for Sound and Vision*)
Kelvin Street (*Librarian*)
Keith Wakeman (*Online Service Administrator*)

Video assets

Nigel Douglas (*Executive Creative Director*)
Robin Tucker (*Head of Production*)

Consultants

James McGill *(Figure descriptions)*
Paul Meakin *(Adviser on Law)*